AMERICA IN HISTORY and BIBLE PROPHECY

AMERICA IN HISTORY and BIBLE PROPHECY

Edited by
DR. THOMAS McCALL

MOODY PRESS
CHICAGO

ISBN: 0-8024-0209-7

Moody Press, a ministry of the Moody Bible Institute, is designed for education, evangelization, and edification. If we may assist you in knowing more about Christ and the Christian life, please write us without obligation: Moody Press, c/o MLM, Chicago, Illinois 60610.

Printed in the United States of America

CONTENTS

INTRODUCTION

America in History and Bible Prophecy is the product of messages delivered and papers read for the Bicentennial Congress on Prophecy during the week of July 4, 1976. Over 40 million people were expected to make a pilgrimage to Philadelphia during the Bicentennial of the Declaration of Independence, and the eyes of the nation and even the world were focused on the city of brotherly love, especially as the Fourth of July drew near. Television, radio, and newspaper coverage was evident all over Philadelphia, with Presidential speeches and parades the order of the day. Many Christians felt that this rare and auspicious occasion should be utilized to stress the spiritual heritage of the Christian faith in our much blessed nation and to strive to spotlight the focus of worldwide interest on the Lord and His Word.

As Conference Director of the American Board of Missions to the Jews, it became my happy assignment to prepare for and organize the Bicentennial Congress on Prophecy in Philadelphia. The Lord gave us a marvelous assemblage of truly outstanding Bible scholars and noted evangelical Christian speakers for the week. Soon, the question was raised as to how significant messages delivered by these remarkable men could be preserved for thousands of interested people who might not be able to attend the Congress. Everyone concerned felt that the timely messages should be published in a book to be made available as soon after the Congress as possible.

America in History and Bible Prophecy contains ten important statements of faith, a challenging barometer of the spiritual life of the church in Bicentennial America, as the kaleidoscopic events of Bible prophecy with Israel on center stage are drawing into ever sharper focus. We commend the book to our readers as an important Declaration of Dependence upon God for our day, and we trust that it will serve to edify the body of Christ, and draw many into the redeeming grace of our Lord Jesus Christ.

THOMAS S. MCCALL

1

AMERICA, CHRISTIANS, AND ISRAEL

John F. Walvoord

From a biblical and divine viewpoint, it is indisputable that Israel occupies a central place in the history of the world. Because of this, it naturally follows that the role of Israel in the history of America becomes important both to our national and religious lives.

Any student of Scripture soon becomes aware of the fact that Israel plays a prominent part in the history of the world from the early chapters of Genesis to the last chapters of the book of the Revelation. Although the nation Israel is comparatively small in number and limited in world influence, in the Bible more space is allotted to the history of Israel and God's dealings with them than to any other subject.

The central place of Israel becomes evident in the study of the book of Genesis. After allocating only two chapters to the whole story of creation and only one chapter to the Fall of man into temptation and sin, the next eight chapters cover the whole history of the world from creation to the time of Abraham. Then, the next thirty-eight chapters deal with the life stories of Abraham, Isaac, and Jacob. To God, Abraham and his descendants are of great importance to the divine program.

The importance and central place of Israel is revealed in the divine covenant with Abraham, recorded in Genesis 12: 1-3 and repeated in various ways throughout the Old Testament. According to this covenant, Abraham was to be a great man, a blessing to the world, and the father of a great nation. While more than one nation would come from Abraham, God had in mind the particular line of descendants through Isaac, Jacob, and Jacob's twelve sons, and the great promises given to Abraham will have their specific fufillment in this line of descendants.

A major consideration in the Abrahamic Covenant is the statement of Genesis 12:3, "And I will bless them that bless thee, and curse him that curseth thee: and in thee shall all families of the earth be blessed." Three important promises are given in this verse. First, God promises to bring special blessing on any nation or people who will be a blessing to Abraham's descendants. Second, God states that He will curse and punish any nation that is Israel's oppressor. Third, through Israel it is God's intent to bring blessing to the entire world.

These promises have already been signally fulfilled in history. God has blessed the nations that have been kind to Israel and has brought severe judgment on those that have been Israel's persecutors, as witnessed in His judgment on Egypt, Syria, Babylon, Rome, Spain, Germany, and Russia. Undoubtedly, one of the reasons why America has been blessed is that it has become a homeland for the Jewish people.

The promise that Israel would be a blessing to the entire world has been graphically fulfilled. Not only have great scientists, mathematicians, and benefactors of the human race come from the nation Israel, but more important, through Israel have come the prophets, the writers of the Old Testament and the New Testament, and preeminently, from Israel has come Jesus Christ, the Saviour of all who trust in Him. Israel, comparatively small among the nations, is central to the eternal purposes of God.

Because of these important factors, it is only natural in reviewing the history of America, to raise the question of the role of the Jew. What has been his history and experience in America? What is the situation today? What is the responsibility of the Christian community to the Jewish community? These are important and searching questions and especially should be considered when reviewing the first 200 years of the history of our United States.

Relation of Israel in America to the Christian Community

One hundred years ago, the Jews of Eastern Europe lived in a world that was hostile. This was not a new experience, because they had suffered greatly at the hands of both Christians and non-Christians through the centuries, to such an extent that, in the Middle Ages, the Jewish population of the world had been reduced to probably less than the number of Jews who left Egypt under Moses. Few islands of tolerance were available to the Jew around the world. Wherever he went, the sad prediction of Moses was fulfilled:

> And the Lord shall scatter thee among all people, from the one end of the earth even unto the other; and there thou shalt serve other gods, which neither thou nor thy fathers have known, even wood and stone. And among these nations shalt thou find no ease, neither shall the sole of thy foot have rest; but the Lord shall give thee there a trembling heart, and failing of eyes, and sorrow of mind. And thy life shall hang in doubt before thee; and thou shalt fear day and night, and shalt have none assurance of thy life: In the morning thou shalt say, Would God it were even! and at even thou shalt say, Would God it were morning! for the fear of thine heart wherewith thou shalt fear, and for the sight of thine eyes which thou shalt see (Deu 28:64-67).

Because of its long history of persecution and the continued attack of the Jew by anti-Semitic governmental decrees, the Jewish community of Europe, especially Eastern Europe, saw in the United States of America a promised land where they could retain their religion and yet have economic, social, and educational opportunities. By 1970, by immigration and multiplication, the Jewish population had reached 6,000,000 and composed three percent of the population of the United States.

But who were the Jews? Although connected by common racial and religious ties, they were divided in their religious, social, and political concepts. The orthodox Jew is marked by continued adherence to the ritualistic religion of his forefathers and the maintenance of his historic faith. The conservative Jew, more flexible than the orthodox, accepted the synagogue, but followed his traditions more loosely. For him, holidays were mostly a festive occasion. The reformed Jew, while recognizing the communal perspective of the Jewish people, regarded as less important the liturgical and theological differences which existed within Judaism and considered them variations in degree and not of kind. The Zionists were occupied with current political, economic, and social problems, and especially with anti-Semitism. Yiddishists were Jews committed to socialism as a way of life, with religion and tradition relegated to the past. A few belonged to the Chasidists, religious revivalists somewhat in revolt and reaction against the cold and rigorous intellectualism of the rabbis. Although just as divided in their basic religious, social, and political concepts as the non-Jewish Gentile world, the American Jew was united by race and history.

The Christian Church's Relation to Israel

Judaism and Christianity have much in common. They share the same Old Testament, and, for many, the same basic convictions about the nature of God. The major difference is the question as to whether Jesus Christ is the Messiah of Israel and the Saviour of the world. Many Jews think that becoming a Christian involves abandonment rather than fulfillment of his religious idealism. Under these circumstances, what has been and what should be the relationship of the Christian Church to Israel?

The relationship between the Church and Israel is undoubtedly colored by the particular convictions of the respective Jew or Christian who might consider the subject. Liberal Christians, with few theological anchors, often find a spiritual affinity with liberal Jews and an open door to share many moral and idealistic convictions. The contrast is much sharper between the orthodox Jew and the orthodox Christian with their more specific theology and the inevitable clash over the question of who is Jesus Christ, and is the New Testament the Word of God? In spite of these deep-seated and significant theological differences, certain attitudes and conclusions emerge for the Christian Church in general in relation to the people of Israel.

First, there is general agreement in America that there should be tolerance of differing religious convictions. Practically all Christians in America, whether liberal or conservative, agree that the Jew should not be forced to confess a faith which is not his and is as free to disbelieve as to believe the Christian Gospel.

It has not always been so, and the sad record of the Inquisitions, where Jews were put to death for refusing to confess Christ, are a great blot on the history of the Church and one which Christians today should unequivocably repudiate. There is no biblical ground for anti-Semitism or intolerance of differing theological concepts in a country that is truly free.

Tolerance, however, is not always enjoyed by either the Jew or the Christian in lands outside the United States. The historic concept of freedom of conscience, one of the great distinctions of the American heritage, is a principle to be jealously guarded and articulately affirmed.

Second, while the Christian Church should continue to confirm tolerance of theological differences in America, this concept does not alter the basic command of Scripture to preach the Gospel to every creature, including the Jew. It is true that Israel in the Old Testament does not seem to have been given a commission to proclaim a universal Gospel to the entire world. The experience of Jonah is clearly the exception rather than the rule.

With the advent of Christ and the revelation of divine salvation in His death and resurrection, the New Testament is plain that a Christian has no alternative. It is God's command that the Gospel be preached throughout the whole world. Christ told His disciples, Jews though they were, "Go ye, therefore, and teach all nations, baptizing them in the name of the Father, and of the Son, and of the Holy Spirit" (Mt 28:19). The final word of Christ as He left His disciples emphasized His point again, "Ye shall be witnesses unto me both in Jerusalem, and in all Judaea, and in Samaria, and unto the uttermost part of the earth" (Ac 1:8). The commission included going to the Jew first, but also to the Gentile. Paul wrote the Romans, "For I am not ashamed of the gospel of Christ; for it is the power of God unto salvation to everyone that believeth; to the Jew first, and also to the Greek. For in it is the righteousness of God revealed from faith to faith; as it is written, The just shall live by faith" (Ro 1:16-17).

The duty of evangelism is bound up in the fact of the absolute necessity of faith in Christ for eternal salvation. As Peter expressed it to the Sanhedrin, "Neither is there salvation in any other; for there is no other name under heaven given among men, whereby we must be saved" (Ac 4:12). The preaching of the Gospel, whether to the Jew or to the Gentile, is not an optional exercise of the Christian Church, but the very heart of its commission.

In modern Christianity, it is not uncommon for Christian liberals, who reject the necessity of the death of Christ and postulate universalism in salvation, to oppose presenting the biblical Gospel to the people of Israel. Likewise, among those who belong to the Jewish community, resentment often has been expressed at Christian attempts to proselyte and convert them to Christianity. The state of Israel, although tolerant of Christian faith, has little patience with the attempts of missionaries to win Jews to Christ. To many Jews, to become a Christian is to betray their own religion and their own race.

In spite of these difficulties, an evangelical Christian has no alternative. We must obey God rather than men. We must proclaim the Gospel whether it is accepted or rejected, whether it is welcomed or resisted. Accordingly, tolerance of Jewish religion in America should not be construed as indifference in regard to the eternal destiny of those who need Christ. The apostles and early Christians faced imprisonment and martyrdom in order to be true to these convictions. In modern America, evangelism has a lower price tag and all the more should be considered as an imperative.

In affirming both tolerance of Jewish religion and the necessity of evangelization of the Jewish people, Christians should leave no question as to their basic opposition to anti-Semitism. There is no biblical basis whatever for hatred of the Jew as a Jew and subjecting the Jew to all types of false propaganda, whether in the political, social, or religious field. The modern Jew, although much opposed to the Christian faith, should have no question in his mind concerning the basic friendliness of the Christian community and the desire of the Church for the Jew to have fair treatment, whether in religious, political, social, or economic situations. Attempts to segregate the people of Israel to certain geographic locations, their exclusion from educational and social organizations, and their boycott in the political arena, conflict with every concept of Scripture which recognizes the dignity and freedom of man, as well as the American principle that all men are created equal.

What Shall We Do?

As the Christian Church faces its obligation in relation to

Israel, it is accordingly clear that there should be no hesitation in presenting the Gospel to them. In these eschatological days, as many see signs of the imminent return of Christ, it is all the more imperative that the Gospel in every way be presented to the Jewish community and that every legitimate form of mission activity should be supported and upheld by the Church.

This is true, even though there is little indication in Scripture that evangelism among the Jews will have outstanding success prior to the coming of Christ for His Church. According to Romans 11:25, when the present age, the time of Gentile blessing, ends with the Rapture of the Church, Israel's eyes will be opened, and many in Israel will turn to Christ. In view of the imminence of Christ's coming, it becomes imperative that every attempt be made to place in the hands of the Jewish community literature which explains both the Old and New Testaments in such a way that those who seek to know the truth will find Christ as their Messiah and Saviour. It is a phenomenon of our age that even in Israel young people are reading the New Testament in their public school education. Many young people in Israel are considering the Gospel with more openness than ever before. Today is a day of opportunity which may suddenly be cut short for the Church in the world. The Church has not only the right, but also the imperative obligation to present the Gospel to the nation Israel.

In asserting its right to preach the Gospel, however, the Christian Church should be most careful to make clear to the people of Israel that they reaffirm their inherent right to religious freedom. The Gospel, imperative as it is in its proclamation, does not achieve its goals by oppression or persecution. The Jew must be loved and appreciated by the Christian, even if he rejects the Christian Gospel. Latent anti-Semitism, born of differing culture, differing religious ideas, and sometimes from the materialism which has engulfed some in Israel, should not stand in the way.

The American Jew should have every reason to believe that the Christian Church is his best friend, that Christians sincerely have Israel's best interest at heart, and that, accordingly, the Christian community stands firmly between the Jew and any repetition of anti-Semitic persecution.

The Christian Church has been generally too silent about the inequities which the Jews face around the world. While much attention has been directed to correcting inequities of blacks and other minorities, too often the Church has been silent when it comes to Jewish prejudices. The whole matter should be reconsidered in the light of the Word of God, which commands the Christian to love not only his friends but also his enemies and to do good to all men. In the light of the sad history of Christian persecution of the Jews in the past, it is all the more important that the Christian today make abundantly clear his attitude of love and appreciation to the Jewish people who, under God, were the original communicators of the Gospel to the Gentile world, through whom the Scriptures have come, and through whom Jesus Christ was born in the flesh. Unquestionably, the future of America and God's blessing upon it continues to depend upon our attitude toward the Jew, and what is true for America is also true for the Church.

2

AMERICA AND THE CAUSE OF WORLD MISSIONS

John F. Walvoord

The Rise of World Missions in America

The history of the United States of America is inseparably related to the cause of world missions. It was only natural that the rising strength of the American colonies in their political and social development should include various types of missionary activity. Many of the early colonists had fled to America from religious oppression abroad and, motivated by deep-seated theological convictions, had come to the new land where the air was free and their conscience unshackled. Some, to be sure, came to seek political freedom itself, and in some cases, desired the freedom of free thinking such as characterized philosophic systems which had cast off the traditional theology of the Church.

Although all forms of religious belief soon appeared in the early life of our country, evident strains of piety, devotion to God, and faith in the Gospel of salvation characterized many. Under the circumstances, it was only natural that, once they were established firmly in their new land, they would become burdened for the spiritual need of their fellow colonists, as well as the Indians.

Some missionary vision was carried over from early missionary interest in England and on the continent. Sometimes this was manifested in prayer groups built on the concept that prayer was the most important means of extension of the Gospel. As early as 1746, a movement was inaugurated to begin a seven-year "concert of prayer" for missionary endeavor. However, the influence of William Carey, who sailed from England for India in June, 1793, soon spread to America.

Among the first to hear the call to preach the Gospel to the world was Samuel J. Mills. Believing that he had been called to carry the Gospel to the entire world, he entered Williams College in 1806 to prepare himself for missionary endeavor. Other students rallied around him, often giving themselves to prayer for the missionary cause. One day, while caught in a sudden thunderstorm, they fled to a haystack where they agreed to be America's first candidates for foreign missionary service. Later, going to Andover Seminary, they were joined by Adoniram Judson and others from neighboring schools, who formed the Society of Inquiry on the Subject of Missions. Gaining the approval of the General Association of the Congregational Ministers of Massachusetts, they formed a foreign missionary board.

The first missionary party consisted of eight missionaries led by Judson. Their sailing ship trip to India took four months. The newly formed missionary society was soon followed by organizations representing the Baptists, Methodists, Episcopals, Protestant Episcopals, Presbyterians, and Evangelical Lutherans.

Meanwhile, extensive missionary efforts were being made at home. Not all the colonists adhered to the Christian faith, and evangelism was the order of the day, even for colonial America. Early missions were also formed to take the Gospel to the Indians, and some of these early missionary efforts to the Indians preceded by more than one hundred years the foreign missionary movement. As early as 1620, colonists set out to convert the Indians. Among the great leaders was John Elliott, who, arriving in America in 1630, combined his work as a Presbyterian pastor in Roxbury, Massachusetts, with missionary work among some twenty tribes in the area. One of the first Bibles printed in America was a translation of the Bible in the Mohican language. Simultaneous with Elliott's ministry were other famous missionaries, including David Brainerd and Henry Martin. The Quakers were especially active in work among the Indians in Pennsylvania and New Jersey.

Early missionary effort also extended to the Blacks, although such activity was often opposed by slave owners at first. As early as 1701, missionary work began among the Blacks, accompanied by increasaing opposition to slavery, especially among the Quakers. As the frontiers moved to the West, missionaries followed the early colonists to bring spiritual influence and the saving Gospel to new communities springing up in the wilderness.

Meanwhile, the cause of world missions continued to advance with American missionaries predominating in Latin America, Indo-China, Burma, Korea, Thailand, Malaya, and the Philippines. Even in Japan, China, and Taiwan, the scene of labors of many European missionaries, Americans represented more than half the missionary force. Likewise in Africa, large sections were evangelized by American missionaries.

In addition to the formation of missionary bodies themselves, certain missionary movements became important, such as the Student Volunteer Movement, the faith mission movement, and the Bible institute movement, which characterized the early twentieth century. Bible institutes were especially productive of missionaries, with Moody Bible Institute sending out over 5,000 missionaries by the midpoint of the twentieth century. Faith missions began to replace many of the denominational mission boards in terms of numbers and influence.

Increasing liberalism in the denominations tended to shrink their missionary efforts, and the combined influence of the Depression and the adverse report of the layman's foreign mission inquiry entitled *Re-Thinking Missions* resulted in many denominational missions reducing their missionary efforts and introducing secularism. The political conditions following World War II were also adverse to missionary activity in some great areas such as China.

In the last twenty years, however, new emphasis for world missions has been provided by various new evangelistic efforts, including extensive Bible translation, youth missionary organization, and great missionary conferences for youth. In the rapidly changing role of the missionary, the cause of world missions dominated by American missionaries may soon take on new characteristics with young churches around the world taking over the missionary task.

To the United States, however, belongs the distinction of providing three-fourths of the missionaries of the last century and approximately the same amount of money and material aid. The cause of world missions has, therefore, been an integral part of the history of America, and, under God, may do much to explain the many blessings which God has showered upon our country.

The Role of America in Fulfilling the Great Commission

As clearly revealed in the Scriptures, the peculiar character of the age following the death, resurrection, and return of Christ to heaven is the command to carry the Gospel to every creature. The disciples were to begin at Jerusalem and spread the Gospel to Judaea, Samaria, and to the world (Ac 1:8). While missionary effort is as old as the Church, and a surprising extension of the Gospel occurred in the first century, it is clear that the twentieth century is a great period of missionary extension. Missionaries have penetrated all the major areas of the world, even though many peoples have still to hear the Gospel. Modern means of communication and transportation, as well as the use of the printed page and production of the Bible in hundreds of new languages, have given wings to the Gospel, such as was impossible before our day. Although millions have not heard the Gospel, probably more have heard the Gospel in the twentieth century than in any preceding period in the history of the Church.

Various missionary organizations are taking seriously the task of taking the Gospel to every creature. While the missionary task has not been limited to missionaries originating in America, the dominant role of the United States in financing and providing personnel for missionary service is evident around the world. Even in a day when liberalism has sapped the missionary zeal of many organizations that once were prominent in missionary extension, God, in His own way, has raised up other organizations and individuals to carry on the work, and the Gospel continues to ring the globe. In many missionary organizations, candidates continue to exceed available funds for expansion of the work.

Relation of World Missions to National Prosperity

The twentieth century saw the rise of the United States to a nation of power and prosperity such as has characterized no previous civilization. Beginning with World War I, the United States tipped the scales in favor of victory for the allies. This was followed by World War II, where the United States rose to its greatest height of international power and influence. The United States has received power and prosperity such as has not yet been enjoyed by any other nation in the history of man. Not only has its power and influence stretched around the world, but its own citizens have enjoyed the fruit of many modern inventions and conveniences. Although America has only seven percent of the world's population, more than half of the modern luxuries that characterize civilization are found in America. The question may fairly be raised as to the reasons for this national prosperity.

It can hardly be said that our United States leads the world in morality or Christian faith. Sadly, all the sins of ancient Rome and Babylon are too often repeated in our own civilization. Although church membership and attendance of church services in America far exceed the countries of Europe from which the colonists came, it is evident that Christianity is a minority belief and that many adherents are only nominal Christians. How, then, can it be demonstrated that America's prosperity is in any sense related to its Christian faith? Although our currency and coins may bear the motto, "In God We Trust," it is clear that this is an empty faith for most Americans.

The answer to the enigma of America's prosperity, in spite of its profligacy of its national resources and its disregard of biblical moral standards, is found by investigating the central purposes of God in the present age. According to Scripture, it is God's central purpose in the present age to preach the Gospel to every creature. In the Old Testament, the working of God was primarily related to Israel, and the history of the world is revealed to revolve around His chosen people. Following Pentecost, it is evident the Gospel was to be carried to every people and tongue. It was God's purpose in this age that the Gospel be preached to everyone.

It is here that the prosperity of America begins its relationship to its program of missionary extension. Although the wealth of America is largely spent on human luxuries and pleasures and comparatively an infinitely small portion of our national wealth has been used for the missionary cause, nevertheless, that which has been used has served to bring the Gospel to the ends of the earth. In the twentieth century, God has prospered America in order to make possible the carrying of the Gospel from American shores to people of every color, race, and culture throughout the world. Just as God has blessed America for its kindness to the Jew in keeping with the Abrahamic promise, so God is using America until now to carry the Gospel to the entire world.

To the superficial observer, America is great because of its resources, its manufacturing capacity, military armament, and its financial power in the world. From a divine standpoint, the prosperity of America stems from its share in fulfilling the program of God in the present age. While few Christians are motivated in their missionary giving by the desire to preserve the freedoms of America and to cause God's continued blessing upon us, undoubtedly, the missionary effort coming from our shores is one of the major reasons why God has blessed us to this hour and withheld so many divine judgments that we undoubtedly deserve as a nation.

According to biblical prophecy, the future of America is not bright. Scriptures predict a world government in the end of the age which will have its center not in America but in the Middle East. The centralization of power which is prophesied as extending to every kindred, tongue, and nation (Rev 13:7) clearly requires that America in that future day lose much of its present strategic place in the world.

How soon this will come no one can predict, but an obvious decisive act of God will be the Rapture of the Church, the catching out of the world of every true Christian. Suddenly evangelical missions will be dissolved. Missionaries will go to their heavenly reward, and the world will be left without its present organized missionary efforts.

Although the Word of God bears witness to a continued testimony to the world after the Rapture, it seems clear that the present means of carrying the Gospel to the ends of the earth will be brought suddenly to their close. When this occurs, it may well be that America not only will lose its political and international leadership, but also will no longer be the first in missionary testimony throughout the world. This serves to confirm the concept that America's missionary program of carrying the Gospel to every creature is today one of God's primary reasons for blessing our great land. The challenge to America is to continue to send forth a stream of young people, using every possible modern means to carry the Gospel to those who have never heard. The task has never been greater or the cause more imperative.

In the future of America, it may well be that the century will witness the decline of America's strength and power. While we yet have the ability and the freedom to send forth ambassadors of the cross, may we do all in our power to extend the Gospel to our generation and fulfill in this way the divine purpose of God to carry the Gospel to every creature.

3

AMERICA AND ISRAEL *versus* WORLD COMMUNISM

W. A. Criswell

> Woe unto them that decree unrighteous decrees, and that write grievousness which they have prescribed; To turn aside the needy from judgment, and to take away the right from the poor of my people, that widows may be their prey, and that they may rob the fatherless! And what will ye do in the day of visitation, and in the desolation which shall come from far? to whom will ye flee for help? and where will ye leave your glory? Without me they shall bow down under the prisoners, and they shall fall under the slain. For all this his anger is not turned away, but his hand is stretched out still. O Assyrian, the rod of mine anger, and the staff in their hand is mine indignation (Is 10:1-5).

For centuries in the ancient world (900, 800, 700, 600 BC), the ruthless, merciless, brutal, and cruel Assyrian Empire held the whole civilized world in an iron hand. Four times in the lifetime of Isaiah the prophet did Assyria overrun Judah, and Assyria destroyed forever the Northern Kingdom of Israel with its capital, Samaria. Ancient Assyria was a veritable ogre to the Jew.

In our modern world, there is an empire far greater, more brutal, more ruthless, more merciless, and it is appeased and accepted by the modern nations of the world. There has never lived an empire so cruel or so oppressive as that of atheistic, Communistic Russia. Her colonies are held in an oppressive and terrible grip. All other modern colonial empires have been liquidated and dissolved. The British Empire is gone. The Dutch Empire is gone. The German Empire is gone. The Italian, the Portuguese—all modern empires—have been liquidated, except this one of Communist Russia. The poor colonies, such as Hungary and East Germany, that are held in an iron vise in her hand, have rebelled four times in desperation. Four times has the Red Army crushed them. Today there are thirty-one Red divisions occupying those nations, lest they rebel again.

How is it that such a blood-thirsty, murderous, torturous, terrible, brutal empire is allowed to exist and to expand among the nations of the modern world? There are two answers.

The Imponderables of Almighty God

One answer lies in the imponderables of Almighty God. When that question was raised in the days of Isaiah, as to why God permitted the brutal and merciless Assyrian Empire to overun the people of God, the Lord sent word through Isaiah to Judah saying, "Assyria is the rod of mine anger and the staff of mine indignation." God raised up the Assyrian Empire to chasten and to punish His people for their sins.

There is a like imponderable today known but to God in heaven. It may be that God allows the ruthless Russian empire to exist in our modern world as a scourge and chastisement of the Christian nations of the West. It is an immoral miracle, Communism.

Once I was a guest in the home of Dr. Black, the President of the Presbyterian Robert College in Istanbul. He had married a Bulgarian. He was in Bulgaria when the Communists took it over. When I asked him how it is that children will inform against their parents, knowing that the parents will be sent to death, he said: "I cannot explain it. It is something in the imponderables of God. As there is a kingdom of light and glory in the earth presided over by Jesus the Son of God, so there is a kingdom of darkness presided over by Satan himself." That is a permissive will and choice that belongs to a mystery in heaven, into which I cannot enter. Why God allows the expansion of Russia as a scourge, as a chastisement of the decline of the Christian faith in the free and Western world, I do not know. Only God knows.

The Immediate Curse of the Left-Winger

But this I can see. I can easily understand the acceptance and expansion of the Soviet empire in the nations of the world by an immediate and patent reason. It lies in the left-winger, in the socialist, in the welfare-stater, in the liberal, in the fellow traveler. Wherever they are in the world—and they are in all of the governments of our Western nations—they are soft toward Communism and easy on Russia. They are always open to governmental planning, to socialism, and to the nationalization of state resources. They are ever eager to support a government that more and more regiments the people and grasps the reins of industry. The only thing that a liberal is against in America, or any of the nations of the world, is the conservative, who believes in work and in paying his debts and in living within his budget.

Look at Britain. Hong Kong is administered by the government of Britain. In 1967, in the terrible riots that tore the city apart, the British government closed down the Communist schools. Since that time, the British government has not only reopened all of those Communist schools but has allowed them to proliferate, and now there are more than seventy Communist schools in Hong Kong alone. These are the schools that are teaching atheism and Communism to the children and high schoolers of Hong Kong.

Missionary Victor Frank, with whom we broke bread, was describing a visit he made in the home of a Chinese family in Hong Kong. They were atheists and announced to the missionary, "We do not believe in God." A little fellow who was in the Communist school spoke up immediately and said: "I believe in God. His name is Chairman Mao Tse-tung." This is the liberal, as he opens the floodgates for the Communist.

While in Great Britain, I listened to the great industrial corporations of England as they made reports to the British people. Night after night, I listened to those reports on television. They have nationalized their industries. They live under a socialist government. I listened to the electric utilities as they reported: every month, millions and millions of pounds in debt. I listened to the coal industry as it reported: every month, millions and millions of pounds in debt. I listened to the steel industry as it reported: every month, millions and millions of pounds in debt. I listened to the transportation industry: millions and millions of pounds in debt. And the taxpayer must pick up the tab. The British government is facing absolute bankruptcy. There is no government that can run an industry profitably. When the government takes it over, when it regulates it, there will soon follow scarcity, want, and finally absolute dissolution.

The Left-Winger Brings Shame to America

The same thing is true in America. The left-winger and the liberal, the fellow traveler, the welfare-stater are the same anywhere you find them in the earth.

For the first time in the history of America (whose glorious two hundred years we are celebrating), we have seen our flag hauled down in defeat and in shame and in ignominy. We have seen the image of the American nation in the dust of the earth, with the result that the isles of the sea and the nations of the world are cowering before the onrush of the Red flood. How did that come to pass?

I will tell you exactly how it came to pass. In the Orient, a man who has lived in Vietnam for years and years, a close friend of General Westmoreland, who headed the armed forces of America in South Vietnam, told me that General Westmoreland said to him: "I could conclude this war in victory in a matter of weeks. All I would need to do would be to take the armies of South Vietnam, our armed forces, and march them to the DMZ and call for the seventh fleet to stand offshore and send word to Hanoi, 'You will either withdraw your forces from South Vietnam or face invasion and annihilation.' The war would then be over overnight." Why wasn't that done? Because of the left-wingers in the United States government, because of the Senate Foreign Relations Committee, and because of various members of Congress and in the Senate who held exactly the same views. They so weakened the power of America to march and to fight for the liberties of our nation and the nations of the world, that we lost the war in disgrace and in shame.

Why should we be afraid of Russia? Russia cannot feed itself. It cannot support itself much less gird itself to sustaining a war to victory. I'm convinced no socialistic system can. Russia is two and one-half times the size of the United States. Russia is forty-five times the size of France. Russia has thirty million farmers. We have six million. I have flown over the great Ukraine from the north to the south and from the east to the west. It comprises thousands of miles of the richest farmland one could ever look upon. Have you ever flown over Wisconsin? Iowa? Illinois? Those are the rich, rolling farmlands that produce the food that America needs. Russia in its Ukraine is exactly like that, rich, productive, and fertile black soil. What's the matter? Why can't it feed itself? It is because of the system. The system will never produce. The system has not produced, and for us to cower before Russia when it cannot feed itself is unthinkable, unimaginable, and cowardly.

What we do is this. We ship our food to Russia. We give them our technological achievements. They cannot excel in any kind of productivity. Russia exists because we sustain and subsidize their failures. Without us they would not exist. They would fall to the ground in a very short while.

In Vietnam, the tanks and the trucks that were used to slay our American boys were made in factories our technicians showed the Russians how to build. The policy of America stated openly and followed undeviatingly is one of appeasement and concession to Russia. It has never deviated from that awesome and tragic course. We think, "Let's feed the wolf and finally he will go away." That has been the constant course of the American government.

Lest We Offend the Russians

There has just come to visit us one of the greatest literary geniuses of our time, Aleksandr Solzhenitsyn. This is a man who believes in God. This is a man who has dared to defy the Kremlin. This is a man who believes that humanity is not a mass of protoplasm, a hunk of evolutionary process, or an animal, but he believes, under God, we are created in His image with sensitivity to right and wrong. This is Aleksandr Solzhenitsyn. The White House and the American government snubbed him. Why? They published a reason blatantly, openly, unashamedly: "We will not invite Aleksandr Solzhenitsyn to the White House or to a public state affair of America because we are afraid of offending the Russians."

This has been our policy through the years. Our armies in victory march before Berlin. We would not dare take it. We might offend the Russians. Churchill said, "For God's sake, invade the soft, underbelly of Europe and let's snatch from them the nations of Eastern Europe." "No," says Franklin Delano Roosevelt, "by no means, lest we offend the Russians."

The Japanese are within a few days of unconditional surrender. We bring in the Russians and give them the northern isles of Japan, lest we offend them in a unilateral victory.

And in this recent war in the Middle East, Israel surrounded completely the army of Egypt. Thereupon the US government sent word to Israel saying, "Withdraw your forces and let the Egyptian army go, lest we offend Russia." This is the policy that governs the life of America; not what we choose, not what we think, but what the Kremlin chooses and what those enigmatic, mysterious, convocations decide on the inside of those high, forbidding walls. And this is detente!

What is detente? Have you read the Helsinki document which the American, Russian, and European leaders signed? Look at what we give. Look at what we concede: (1) Forever we concede to Russia 182,000 square miles—not acres—182,000 square *miles*—of the land of Eastern Europe that belonged to Finland, Poland, and Romania. The borders of Russia have been extended westward into the very heartland of Central Europe. That we signed in detente. What else did we give in detente? (2) We forever obliterated the little nations of Estonia, Latvia, and Lithuania. They are now, by our decree and our signature, forever lost, swallowed up in the ravages of the Russian empire. That we did in detente. Something else (3) Forever, we said, the nations of Eastern Europe are colonies of Russia. The boundaries are set. They belong to the Russian Communist Kremlin rulers. In defeat and in despair, we have assigned them forever to a life of misery and of oppression. That we did in detente. What did Russia concede to us? What did we gain by signing that document? We gained something like this: (1) If there is a son or a daughter on this side of the iron curtain, he may have the privilege, under certain circumstances, of visiting his relative. (2) Under certain conditions, a correspondent, on the other side of the wall, can come out and look at us.

That is it! My brother, every one of those things are

basic, human rights: the right to visit a family and the right to look at another people, nation, and government. By detente, we concede basic human rights to the Russian government, and in return we forever give away the people who live in despair in Eastern Europe. That is detente!

When you look at the future, what does it hold for us and for the nations of the world? The Red menace spreads and spreads and spreads. It is a story familiar now in India, in Portugal, in the nations of Africa, in South America, and around the whole earth. Does the future belong to them? Do we cringe and die in fear and foreboding before it? Is that the way of tomorrow?

In Hyde Park in London, I listened to a Communist on a tall stepladder with a platform, with a big red flag flying above him. He mouthed the platitudinous axioms of Karl Marx. I wish I had time to repeat some of them, just to show you how ridiculous they are and how oppressive they are in the life of the people. As he was mouthing them up there, the people were heckling him from every side. That is the privilege in Hyde Park. As he was storming about the glories of Communism, one of the fellows spoke up and said, "Tell me, explain to us the anti-Semitism of Karl Marx. Do that if you can." He stumbled around because there is no answer. Then another heckler said, "You up there, you with the red flag, tell us about the murders of the millions who were butchered by Joseph Stalin. Tell us." He mouthed something about that. Then another heckler spoke up and said, "You tell us about that wall in Berlin and the Iron Curtain that separates the people." He mouthed something about that. So they were heckling him on every side. Finally the fellow came to a peroration, and this is what he said: "The wave of the future belongs to us. We shall have revolution in every nation of the earth, liberating the oppressed working mass. It has happened in Russia. It has happened in China. It has happened in Vietnam. It has happened in Cuba. It is happening in the nations of Africa and South America, in Portugal and in India. The only one that could intervene is the United States of America, and he is somewhere playing some kind of a game called mumbo-jumbo." When he said that, you would have thought there would have been 500 hecklers stand up and say, "That's a lie, that's a lie, that's a Communist lie." But there was absolute silence. There was not a man or a woman who said anything.

What would you say? He said that it happened in Cuba, in Vietnam, in the nations of the world, and the United States is off to the side playing some kind of mumbo-jumbo. You bow your head and pray to God. Is that true? If it is, if the wave of the future is theirs, then it means the loss of human freedom and the destruction of the home and the family. It means the annihilation of the Church, and it means the extermination of the people of God. Is that what we see in God's world where we live?

The Christian and the Communist

We have an answer from the Holy Scriptures and from the holy prophets. A vast, indescribable destruction awaits the nation of Russia. God will judge and will destroy those people who mock His name and who teach their children that He does not exist. That annihilation will come to pass when the Red Communists attack Israel.

Dr. Thomas S. McCall and Rev. Zola Levitt have written of that coming Russian invasion in their exposition of Ezekiel, chapters 38 and 39, in their book, *The Coming Russian Invasion of Israel.* It is truly a terrible thing to fall into the hands of the living God.

We have an answer from heaven. Along with those visiting Lenin's tomb in the Red Square before those Kremlin walls, I lined up and finally made my way to the tomb. On the right side, on the lower side, and on the left side, you look into the dead and silent face of Nickolai Lenin. He died in 1924 at the age of fifty-four. His death came as a shock to the Communist world. When he died, the Grand Presidium of the Supreme Soviet of Russia gave the announcement to the world, and I quote it verbatim. The Grand Presidium said: "No man ever wrought as Lenin. He was the greatest teacher of all time. He was the greatest leader among men. He was the author of a new social order. He was the saviour of the world." But he is dead! As I walked on this side and that side and the other side, I turned over in my mind that pronouncement of the Supreme Soviet, "He was the greatest teacher, the greatest leader, the author of the new social order, he was the saviour of the world." But he is dead. Look at him. He is still and silent in death. Unknown to the Grand Presidium, unknown to the Supreme Soviet that sits in the Kremlin, they spelled their ultimate defeat in the very tense of the word that they used. "He *was* the greatest teacher." But he is dead. "He *was* the greatest leader." Dead. "He *was* the author of a new social order." Dead. "He *was* the savior of the world." He is dead. Look at him.

But with what glory and with what triumph does the Christian stand in this dark world, raise his voice and lift his face toward heaven and say, "Christ is alive!" He was raised from the dead! There is no tomb before any wall which you can visit and say, "There Christ is buried." Why not? Because He is alive, and He reigns in heaven, and someday He shall reign in earth. He is, He is, He is! He *is* the greatest teacher of all time. He *is* the greatest Leader among men. He *is* the Author of a new social order. He *is* the Saviour of the world. He *is* our coming, reigning King.

This morning I met a couple. They have just come back from Russia. As upon me, so upon them, the Christians gathering in the Baptist Church in Moscow made a profound impression, weeping, crying, with hands uplifted to God. There is just one church for a city of seven million people. It is allowed to be a showcase for the tourists who thereby are persuaded of the religious freedom in Russia. The worshipers in this Russian church are hurt and oppressed, and you see it in their faces and lives. But they have a choir that sings gloriously. They were singing a song that day I was there. It has a triumphant note in it. There were only three words that I could recognize: *Iesous, Christus,* and *Hallelujah* (a word that denotes praise to God in all languages of the world). I turned to the Russian minister seated next to me in the pulpit and said, "What are they singing about?" He said, "They are singing about the second coming of Christ, the triumph of our Lord when He comes again."

Jesus shall reign where'er the sun
Shall his successive journeys run.
His kingdom spread from shore to shore
Till moons shall wax and wane no more.
"Jesus," "Christ," "Hallelujah."

All hail the power of Jesus' name,
Let angels prostrate fall;
Bring forth the royal diadem,
And crown Him Lord of all.
"Jesus," "Christ," "Hallelujah."

Lo! He comes with clouds descending,
Once for favored sinners slain,
Thousand, thousand saints attending
Swell the glory of His train.
Hallelujah, hallelujah God appears on earth to reign.
"Jesus," "Christ," "Hallelujah."
Come, blessed Saviour.

When He comes, there will be a people to welcome Him and to receive Him in the earth. Oh, what a faith, what a commitment, what a love, what a triumph, what an optimism! What an indomitable and indestructible spirit! The victory belongs to the people of God.

Our honorable Congressmen, may there be others who stand by your side as you seek to bring America back to the foundations upon which it was built by our forefathers. And please, God, hand it down to our children without shame and disgrace.

God bless America.

4

THE SPIRITUAL FOUNDATIONS OF AMERICA

W. A. Criswell

Many millions of us look with pride upon our American nation and remember our national history. I was brought up to love and to respect our flag and the country for which it stands. I was taught to reverence our godly traditions. There is still a poignant feeling in my heart and there are still tears in my eyes when I see Old Glory unfurled over the Capitol building or flying over a military cemetery or carried by a soldier in a parade on a city street.

> Hats off! Along the street there comes
> A blare of bugles, a ruffle of drums
> A flash of color beneath the sky
> Hats off! The flag is passing by.
>
> Sign of a nation great and strong
> To ward her people from foreign wrong
> Honor and glory and power all
> Live in the colors to stand or fall.
>
> Hats off! Along the street there comes
> A blare of bugles, a ruffle of drums
> And loyal hearts are beating high
> Hats off! The flag is passing by.

Any time I go abroad, it is still with prayers and deepest gratitude for America that I come back home. I remember one time returning from a four-month's mission tour around the world. Late at night, the plane was approaching the shores of our country. I cannot forget the thrill I felt when the pilot announced, "The next lights you see will be the shores of America."

We share the patriotic sensitivity of Sir Walter Scott in his, "Lay of the Last Minstrel."

> Breathes there the man with soul so dead,
> Who never to himself hath said,
> "This is my own, my native land"
> Whose heart hath ne'er within him burned
> As home his footsteps he hath turned
> From wandering on a foreign strand?

This is our America, the land of our fathers and the land of our love.

It is a nation built around the church and founded upon the Chrisitan faith.

Every schoolchild knows that the Spanish conquistadores came to the New World seeking gold, while the Pilgrims came to the shores of America seeking the will of God. Praying for freedom from oppression, they came here to build the Christian home, the Christian church, and the Christian school, where the Bible was taught in all its meaning and glory.

In the founding of the great American nation, our Christian forefathers had a mighty and worthy part. One hundred forty-seven years before the signing of the Declaration of Independence, 153 years before William Carey inaugurated the modern mission movement, 206 years before the Southwest became a part of the United States, our little churches and their faithful preachers began the evangelization of the frontier facing the wild wilderness. Our churches grew afar. There were no missionary organizations. The incessant, unwearying evangelization was the work of men who were not sent forth, but who went forth to preach in obedience to a divine call.

History and the historian recount the heavenly blessing of God upon their dedicated efforts.

As the population extended over the Alleghenies into the new regions of the great West, the missionary zeal of the churches kept step with the colonizing enterprise of the people.

Men of God went forth into this wilderness not knowing where they should find a night's lodging or their next meal, willing to suffer untold privations if they might only point some to the Lamb of God. It is impossible to estimate too highly or to praise too warmly these men of strong faith and good works. Their hardships were such as we of the present day can hardly imagine. They traveled from little settlement to settlement on horseback, with no road save an Indian trail or blazed trees, fording streams over which no bridges had been built. They were exposed to storms, frequently sleeping where night found them, often prostrated by fevers or wasted by malaria, but indomitable still. If they did not wander "in sheepskins and goatskins" like ancient heroes of faith, they wore deerskins. Homespun took the place of sackcloth. Their dwelling was "all out o' doors." Living in the plainest manner, sharing all the hardships of a pioneer people, the circuit preacher labored in a parish that, as one of them said, "took in one-half creation, for it had no boundary on the west." One of them writes in 1806:

> Every day I travel I have to swim through creeks or swamps, and I am wet from head to feet; and some days from morning to night I am dripping with water. . . . I have rheumatism in all my joints. . . . What I have suffered in body and mind my pen is not able to communicate to you. But this I can say: While my body is wet with water and chilled with cold, my soul is filled with heavenly fire; and I can say with Paul: "But none of these things move me, neither count I my life dear unto myself, so that I might finish my course with joy."

For the most part, the preacher was kindly received, often with tears of joy. The people who were facing death by starvation or freezing had not much to give the itinerant minister. Even to offer him food and shelter meant sacrifice, but in nearly every case, he was welcome to his share of whatever comforts the pioneer family possessed. In the wilderness, like Paul, he passed through many perils, perils from savage beasts, perils from godless and degraded men. But God, who closed the mouths of the lions was with his servant, the pioneer preacher.

The houses of worship in which these preachers held their services were generally God's own temples—the woods and prairies. Their libraries consisted of a Bible and a hymnbook, carried in their saddlebags. The preaching was of a rough-and-ready sort, not always scrupulous of the king's English, but strongly tinged with the good old doctrines of grace, eminently evangelistic, and richly blessed of God to the conversion of their hearers. These men, uncouth as they would seem now, unwelcomed as they would be to the pulpit of any fashionable church, led multitudes to the cross of Christ, founded churches in all the new communities of the West, laid the foundations of denominational institutions on which a magnificent superstructure has since been built. We who have entered into the labors of such men are noble indeed, if we are worthy to unloose the latchet of their shoes.

The nation that they built is the greatest, noblest, freest, richest on earth.

What makes a nation great? If continental expanse made a nation great, Siberia would be the mightiest country on the face of the globe. If concentrated population made a nation great, India would be the greatest nation in the world. If ancient culture made a nation great, China would be the leader of all the families of men. What makes a nation great? It is the character of the people. A nation is made great, not by its fruitful acres, but by the men who till them; not by its great forests, but by the men who use them; not by its rich mines, but by the men who work them; not by the vast systems of transportation, but by the men who build them. As Lyman Abbott said: "America was a great land when Columbus discovered it. Americans have made of it a great nation."

Stretching from side to side, wide as the continent is wide, from ocean to ocean, America is not only a land of charm, beauty, wealth and resources, emerald forests, mighty mountains, broad plains, teeming cities, and winding rivers, but it is also a land of freedom, churches, schools, and godly homes.

> O beautiful for spacious skies,
> For amber waves of grain,
> For purple mountain majesties
> Above the fruited plains!
>
> America! America!
> God shed His grace on thee,
> And crown thy good with brotherhood
> From sea to shining sea.

America is worth winning. It is worth saving. It is worth evangelizing. It is worth preaching to. It is worth dying for.

Who will possess it? It will be us of the Christian faith or someone else. When Alexander the Great lay dying, his generals asked him, "Sir, whose is the kingdom?" The world conqueror replied, "It is for him who can take it!"

What of the future of our beloved country? "Watchman, what of the night?"

Whether we live or die lies in the imponderables of Almighty God. America cannot survive in wickedness, drunkenness, debauchery, and open shame. If the forces of violence, blasphemy, and darkness win our nation, we are lost, eternally, tragically, forever lost. Long ago the ancient psalmist said, "The wicked shall be turned into hell, and all the nations that forget God!" (Ps 9:17). And Rudyard Kipling, a modern prophet, added in his poem "Recessional":

Far-called our navies melt away,
On dune and headland sinks the fire
Lo, all our pomp of yesterday
Is one with Ninevah and Tyre!
Judge of the Nations, spare us yet,
Lest we forget—lest we forget!

If, drunk with sight of power we loose
Wild tongues that have not thee in awe—
Such boasting as the Gentiles use,
Or lesser breeds without the Law—
Lord God of hosts, be with us yet,
Lest we forget, lest we forget!

The forces of evil and the powers of darkness are riding hard to seduce our nation into secularism and materialism, leaving God out of human life. If they succeed, if they win, we have lost our country. Secularism is the same all over the world, whether here or in Communist Russia. Godlessness is the same, whether here or in Hanoi. Blasphemy and impiety and sacrilege are the same, whether here or in Red China. The difference, ultimate and final, between the slavery of the Communist world and freedom of the Western world is God. If we lose His presence and blessing, we have lost all we hold dear to the conquest of a merciless and ruthless enemy. Our homes, our families, our churches, our nation shall have fallen prey to the cruel captivity of darkening forces that are anti-God, antichurch, anti-Christ, and antireligion. The only compelling and intense power that stands between us and the loss of our souls and of our nation is that represented by the Church of the Lord Jesus Christ.

This is the tragedy of all tragedies. At a time when the Church ought to be at her best, she is at her worse. In a day when she ought to confront the world in strength, she is herself weakened by anemia. I was appalled to read in the newspaper of one Dallas-area church which allowed a stripper to "do her own thing" in a morning so-called worship service.

Now let us look in sorrow at a recent article. The cold, brutal fact was editoralized by Jack Harwell, editor of the Georgia *Christian Index* in these words:

> One year ago, we editorially told you about a national magazine survey which rated "organized religion as the 18th resident on a list of the 18 most influential institutions in the United States. Many of you wrote your shock at such a finding.
>
> Well, that same magazine, *U. S. News and World Report* published a new survey in its April 21 issue this year. It listed the 24 "most powerful institutions in the U. S." and organized religion had dropped to 23rd on the tally. Not a single religious leader was listed among the 19 most influential Americans in 1975.
>
> Such a survey speaks volumes to Christians. There's a big world outside the walls of our churches. Other people are shaking that world because Christians are forsaking that world. What will the 1976 survey reveal?

We need a call to arms. We need a rebirth of the sacred purposes inculcated within us when we looked in saving faith to the Lord Jesus Christ. It was His intent that the world would be evangelized through His Church. To her was given the Great Commission. There was no other agency in His mind, nor in the mind of the apostles, when the heavenly mandate was laid upon us. We cease to be the Church of the Lord when we cease to obey the injunction to evangelize.

When I wrote the book, *Why I Preach That the Bible Is Literally True,* some bitter critics avowed that I had set the churches back twenty years. I would to God I could have set it back 120 years to the days of the great revivals under Finney and Moody. I would to God I could have set it back 220 years to the Great Awakening under Jonathan Edwards and George Whitfield and John Wesley. I would to God I could have set it back 2000 years to the day of the great Pentecostal revival under Simon Peter and John, the Son of Zebedee; yea, back 2030 years to the first showing of John, the son of Zacharias, preaching in the wilderness of Judea, and saying, "Repent ye, for the kingdom of heaven is at hand" (Mt 3:2). Our nation needs a revival, a turning to Christ!

When I was a boy, we lived on a farm just beyond the far west Texas line in New Mexico. We lost everything we had in the drought of the dust bowl. I have seen the sky turn to brass and the earth to iron. I have heard the cattle lowing for water. I have seen the pastures from horizon to horizon filled with barren waste and empty sand. I have seen families suffer in penury and want.

One day, as a little, little boy, I was standing in the back door of our farmhouse with my father. To my amazement, he began to shout at the top of his voice. My father by nature was quiet and reserved. To see him shout at the top of his voice was an amazement to me. I looked up to him and said, "Daddy, what are you shouting for? What are you shouting for?" My father replied, "Son, the rain! The rain! God has given us rain!" The falling rain meant bread to our hungry mouths and clothes to our naked backs. It meant life to the family.

We need that falling, heavenly, life-giving visitation from above.

Oh, for the floods on the thirsting land,
Oh, for a mighty revival.
Oh, for a fearless, sanctified band,
Ready to hail its arrival.

The need of the land is revival,
A freshet of grace from above.
Repentance toward God and forgiveness,
More trusting in Christ and his love.

The need of the church is revival,
More prayers for those who are lost.
More fulness of spirit in witness,
More zeal without counting the cost.

Are you the pastor of a church? Are you a leader in a church? Are you a denominational servant of an association of churches? Are you a member of a church? The urgency of the mandate of Christ to make known the Gospel to every creature is addressed to you. There is no discharge for even the least of us from that assignment. Every Christian is summoned to duty. We all have been called to this soul-winning dedication. The total mobilization of the total Church for the total task of winning America to Christ is our God-given goal.

Evangelism comes out of the heart of our people and out of the health of our churches. We cannot give what we do not possess. Where there is life and health in the Church, growth and evangelism inevitably follow. When the root of the tree is strong in doctrine, in faith, and in commitment, the fruit of the branch is abundant in life-giving salvation.

The soul-winning revival must begin in us. Judgment always begins at the house of the Lord. The stinging rebuke of one of our Christian leaders is all too true: "Too long we have been in the position of wanting to enjoy something without enduring something; of wanting to possess something without being something, of wanting to have something without doing something."

When our fellowship is real with the touch of God upon it, when our hearts are filled with the love of the Lord and of the people for whom He died, when it is a concern to us whether men are lost or saved, then the Almighty will hear our prayers from heaven, and will heal our land from evil. Then, if it be, as Jesus reported, that in heaven is rejoicing over the repentance of one sinner, how much more shall we rejoice over a whole nation that turns to God? Help us, Master, to win our America to Christ.

5

THE CONTRIBUTION OF HEBREW CHRISTIANITY TO AMERICA

Charles L. Feinberg

If it can be validly maintained that the debt of America to the Jewish heritage is an area little known among the general populace, then it is all the more certain that the contribution of Hebrew Christianity to America is a *terra incognita* to the world of professing Christians. Once the story is told, even in its broadest outlines, it staggers the imagination with its tremendous ramifications for the cause of Christ at home and abroad. Among the several ways of approach to this vital theme, perhaps the easiest and most interesting is that of the biographical and autobiographical treatment. Among the plethora of cases, time places severe limitations upon us to be selective. Obviously, the choices will be arbitrary, but a controlling factor will be the breadth and depth of influence exerted in each case for the cause of Hebrew Christian witness throughout America and the world as well.

Philipp Philips

As in the first century of the Christian witness, so ever since, there have been rabbis who have accepted Jesus of Nazareth as their personal Saviour and Messiah and have left their mark on their generation and followers by their devotion and service to Him. One such was Philipp Philips. He was blessed, as many Jews have been, by being born in a godly home. At an early age he became acquainted with the literature of the Jews. He later became rabbi of a synagogue in New York City.

One Friday evening he entered the synagogue just at the moment that the cantor was singing the words: "O Bridegroom, meet the Bride; let us go forward to bring in the Sabbath. . . . Arise from the dust. Put on your beautiful garments, My people; through the son of Jesse from Bethlehem comes salvation to my soul."

Philips longed earnestly for salvation. His heart, however, was full of fear that he might not be saved. He took refuge in his books; he read all the Jewish writings, the Mishna and the Gemara; the Midrash Rabba and the Targum, an Aramaic translation of the Bible; and numerous other writings. Yet nothing was able to satisfy the longing of his heart; nowhere could he get information on the matter. In whom could he confide? He was unable to think of any member of his congregation who was competent to help him. Besides, there was the possibility that he might be suspected of wanting to forsake the Jewish religion.

Now it so happened that during that time of fear and doubt, the converted Rabbi Jacob Freshman was working in New York. He was the director of a mission to the Jews. It was his privilege to lead many Jewish souls to the Saviour through his earnest ministry. Philips felt attracted to this man, but he did not risk going to him during the day. He knew it was dangerous for him to visit such a man openly. Consequently, he decided to go late at night.

On his way, Philips met the well-known evangelist D. L. Moody, with whom he had been friendly for a long time. They greeted each other warmly, and, with surprise, Mr. Moody asked Philips, "Rabbi, what compels you to go out so late in the night?"

Philips told him that he was on the way to the Reverend Freshman.

"He is away on a mission tour," said Moody, "and he will probably be gone for a couple of weeks." Then, as Philips recounted, Moody continued, "Rabbi, why do you not stay at home and enjoy the fruit of your table? Friend, you are restless; I can notice that. My spirit tells me you are a Nicodemus." At once he saw that he had said the right thing, and rejoiced: "Praise the Lord!" Moody told him also that he and Dr. Rosvally, a well-known physician, had prayed for his conversion. He requested him to read the New Testament, but Philips refused because he was afraid the Jewish people would persecute him should they hear of it. Moody, however, was not easy to get rid of. He offered the rabbi a New Testament which he had with him, asking Philips to read the first chapter of the gospel of Matthew. Still he refused, claiming it would be impossible for him to believe in the Jesus of Moody. But in the end he accepted the Book.

And what a discovery he made then! He had thought to find a fountain of pride, selfishness, hatred, and violence; instead he found only love, humility, and peacefulness. Instead of stones he found pearls; where he was afraid of thorns, roses spread their fragrance; where he thought to read of life's burden, there he read of blessedness, resurrection, and heavenly treasures. Now he could understand the narratives of the Old Testament in the grand light of the New. As God had led the fathers in the wilderness, so he saw Jesus as the Guide to lead us on the way of salvation. Philips realized that the half had not been told him. He was converted to Jesus as his Saviour and Lord. He saw Jesus as the Redeemer of Israel and the whole human race. He trusted God's promises implicitly, and could at last understand the words of Isaiah 53:4-5: "Surely he hath borne our griefs, and carried our sorrows: yet we did esteem him stricken, smitten of God, and afflicted. But he was wounded for our transgressions, he was bruised for our iniquities: the chastisement of our peace was upon him; and with his stripes we are healed."

Soon he was being persecuted greatly. His friends did not understand him; his profession of the Christian faith was put down to blindness; people asked him how much money he had been paid to become a Christian. All this caused him a great deal of pain. But he knew that he could not expect anything else. The hardest blow came from his mother, who wrote him: "Philipp! You are no longer my son. We have buried you figuratively. You have deserted your father's religion and the synagogue for the deceiver, Jesus, and therefore a curse will be upon you." The letter wounded him deeply.

The more his people hated and despised him, the more fervently he loved them and prayed for them. After three weeks he was able to send his mother a kind, loving reply to her letter, and could only long for the day when he would be able to take the message of Calvary to his dear ones. His one desire was to become a minister and preach the Gospel of Jesus Christ, a desire realized through the help of God. He served his Master faithfully for many years.

Isidor Loewenthal

The Eastern midnight stillness was broken by the firing of a pistol. The morning revealed the lifeless form within the mission compound.

Isidor Loewenthal was scarcely thirty-seven; his term of service in the East just nine years. Yet he has been called "one of the most remarkable men India has ever known." Killed by a shot from the pistol of his own watchman, an ardent Moslem, Loewenthal's dreams of winning Afghanistan for Christ seemed at an end, but death could not stop such a lifework as his.

Men carried him back to his room. It was a student's room, lined with books from floor to ceiling, rare copies of books in many tongues, considered the most priceless collection of Asiatic manuscripts ever found in the hands of a private person. On his desk lay the almost completed manuscript of his Pushtu dictionary; copies of his other works in that language; and above all, his crowning gift to the people of the Afghan land—the New Testament in Pushtu, the common language of its millions.

Though he was less than a decade in the East, men of the highest rank in civil and military life came to him for counsel and friendship. Socially, he was a delightful member of any group. Few men knew better than he the customs of the people he contacted, or were more conversant with Oriental politics . His mastery of music, mathematics, and metaphysics was phenomenal. His sharp mind penetrated the intricate religions of the East. As a disputant with those who professed them, whether Moslem, Brahmin, or Buddhist, he was always the master.

The now silent lips had proclaimed God's message in many tongues: Pushtu, Hindustani, Persian, Cashmere, Arabic, dialects of northern India, Hebrew, English, German, and French.

He had known pain and tragedy; his parents had spurned him because he chose Jesus Christ as Messiah and Saviour. It is a far path from that Indian grave to the Orthodox Jewish home in Posen, Prussian Poland where Isidor Loewenthal was born. When he graduated from Gymnasium at seventeen, his father decided his education was enough for him to enter business. Isidor obeyed with regret, but his beloved books took all his spare hours, even into the night. In time his father was convinced that Isidor's field was that of knowledge. Plans were being made for his study at one of the German universities when the first change in his life came suddenly.

Political dissent had run riot among German students. Young Loewenthal portrayed the spirit of the times in a satirical poem which, unintentionally on his part, appeared in one of the public journals. When he learned that it was being vindictively traced to him, he hastily made his escape, via Hamburg, to America.

In this strange country, with little financial means and less knowledge of the language, Isidor found life very hard. One by one his dreams were dashed to the ground. He found no place in New York or Philadelphia. He decided to try the country, but when the sturdy farmers saw his small frame, they turned him away. He turned to peddling. One rainy night found him in Rockford, a little town near Wilmington, Delaware. At one home, a kindly lady invited him in from the rain while she made her choice from his wares. When he was about to leave, a friendly voice from upstairs called, "Wait, come in, get dry and warm and stay and eat with us. It's a terrible night."

When they talked later around the fire, the Rev. S. M. Gayley, pastor of the Rockford Presbyterian Church, was surprised to find his guest a master of languages and a man of wide learning. The pastor and his wife made a home for the young man. At the family altar the next morning, Isidor courteously bowed his head and heard the first Christian prayer in his life. Gayley soon found a position for him as a teacher of French and German in Lafayette College.

The radiance of the lives of that home deeply impressed the young man and demanded some explanation. Secretly, he began to study the New Testament; openly he tried to master English, often studying the whole night.

At Lafayette a new friend came into Loewenthal's life. He was a Jew, but a Jew who was eager to serve the Christ he avowed. Victor Herschell became Loewenthal's roommate. Both were versed in the Talmud; beyond the midnight hours they discussed the claims of Christ. Herschell's faith and life, however, were his most impressive argument. How was Loewenthal to explain Herschell, a cultured, astute man of his own nation?

After a long inward struggle, Loewenthal yielded allegiance to Christ, accepting Him as Messiah and Saviour. He wrote

Gayley that through faith in the Messiah, he was not only a son of Abraham, but truly a son of God. In the autumn of that year he made a public profession of faith, was baptized, and became a member of the Rockland Church. He continued to teach and pursued his language studies until he decided to enter theological seminary. He was graduated from Princeton Theological Seminary with highest honors, and was appointed the essayist of his class at the commencement. He wrote an essay entitled, "India as a Field of Labor."

He tutored in college for a brief time, during which calls came to fill pulpits. But he longed to reach out to those who did not know Christ. Soon after he was licensed and ordained as a missionary to India, he set sail for the East.

Arriving at Rawalpindi, north of Lahore, his first task was to begin the study of the necessary language. But which one? Three faced him: Hindustani, used by officials; Persian, spoken by the aristocracy; and Pushtu, the common language of Afghanistan. He decided to master them all and added Arabic for religious discussions with Moslems. It was easier by far to climb the mountains into the interior of the land than to conquer the intricacies of the Afghan language. He set out to blaze a trail.

After a short stay in the city, Loewenthal wrote, "Peshawar is the Gibraltar of the East, where Jew and Gentile, exiled Europeans and refugee Asiatics, Bengalis and cutthroat Afghans meet and jostle one another. The surrounding scenery is full of grandeur." He longed to pass beyond and be almost the first to proclaim the news of salvation through the Lord Jesus Christ to the remotest border of the forbidden land, a land some thirty-three thousand square miles larger than France, with a population that exceeded that of France by almost 150 million.

While he waited for the opening of the land, he envisioned that where he might not go, a Pushtu translation of the New Testament could penetrate. Without knowledge of grammar or possession of a dictionary, he set to work on the language, speaking with the learned and testing on the unlearned. He polished, revised, and perfected. He wrote to a friend: "Events which may take the most sagacious statesmen and diplomats by surprise may furnish the key and suddenly the gates may burst open. At that moment let the Church be ready to go in and possess . . . what is civilization without the Gospel?" With the New Testament, the Spirit of God could speak to the highest and lowest of the Afghans. Though he could not cross the borders to preach, many came to him on the India side; traders, learned Mullahs, zealous Imans, respectable Khans. They often took home with them the gift of all gifts, the story of Christ in their own tongue.

Daily he could be seen in the shade of the mosque with Afghans pressing close to him. Bravely he went to sow the seed. The debates may have seemed fruitless, yet they won him respect and friendship. And just when he began to sense possibilities, there came the open grave. Dr. Samuel Zwemer said: "For the evangelization of the Mohammedan world we need first and, most of all men, the best men the Church can afford—men, who, in the spirit of Isidor Loewenthal hold not their lives dear; men who carry the burden of those millions of Moslems upon their hearts, and with Abraham of old, cry out, 'O that Ishmael might live before thee.' " What an inestimable contribution to America and the world did Hebrew Christianity make in the life and labors of Isidor Loewenthal!

Solomon L. Ginsburg

"To whom does the prophet refer in this chapter?" It was the question from a boy of fourteen to his father, a rabbi. The rabbi and his followers were celebrating the Feast of Tabernacles. The boy had opened a copy of the prophets at a passage evidently often examined, chapter 53 of Isaiah. The boy repeated the question to his father. Quiet fell on the company. When the lad repeated his question, the father, in confusion seized the book and slapped his son in the face—an excellent way, surely, to fix an idea in the mind of the boy.

In such an Orthodox home, Solomon L. Ginsburg was born in Suwalki, Poland. At six he was sent to his mother's native city, Koenigsberg, Germany, to get a better education than was available for a Jewish boy in Poland. His mother's father was a wealthy, learned, widely traveled merchant, who took the boy with him often on his journeys.

At fourteen, his father insisted he return to Suwalki. Solomon revolted at the rigid traditional Judaism at home. Moreover, his father wanted him to be a Jewish teacher. The plan included marriage to the daughter of a wealthy Jewish family. Since his bride was twelve and he was fifteen, and the wedding was being prepared without his wishes being consulted, he ran away.

After many experiences he came to London, where his mother's brother took him in and employed him in his large dry-goods store. Here his life was changed. Walking through the Whitechapel district one Jewish Sabbath afternoon, he met a missionary to the Jews who invited him to the Mildmay Mission to the Jews to hear him explain Isaiah 53. At once the incident which occurred during the Feast of Tabernacles when he was fourteen came before him. Curious, he decided to go.

At the mission, he did not understand all the interpretation, but a deep impression was made on him. His subsequent reading of the New Testament convinced him that Jesus of Nazareth was truly the Messiah of his people. He struggled for three months, counting the cost of declaring his faith. At a meeting where John Wilkinson of the Mildmay Mission spoke on Matthew 10:37: "He that loveth father or mother more than me is not worthy of me," the words went right to his soul. Finally completely convinced, he arose and said with trembling voice: "I want to be worthy of Jesus." Joy, peace, and forgiveness flooded his soul, and tears of happiness flowed.

The next morning his uncle asked him the reason for his radiant face, and Solomon told him of the struggle, ending with the decision he had made. When efforts to change his mind failed, he was driven from the home without his belongings. For a year he heard nothing from his people. Then his father's brother came to London to dissuade him from his so-called apostasy. He had to decide between his new belief, and excommunication and disinheritance. He was given a week for the decision—a long, trying, agonizing week. When his uncle, along with several elders of Israel, pleaded with him to renounce the faith, he refused. So they cursed him. In his mind he visualized the Messiah bearing the curse for him on the cross.

At once Ginsburg began to tell others the news of salvation. He was repeatedly stoned, knocked down, kicked, and injured until unconscious. After three years in the printers' trade and another three years in a training college, he answered the call to missionary service in Brazil, the largest political division of the Western hemisphere—larger than the US without Alaska, and sixty-five times the size of England. He was sent to Portugal to study the language. By the end of the first month in Portugal, he had written a tract in English, translated it into Portuguese, had it printed, and went about the country selling it.

His labors in Brazil read like modern chapters in the Acts of the Apostles. He decided to follow Paul's example in confirming new converts. God used him to found scores of churches in different areas of Brazil. In some centers as many as a thousand persons were won to Christ in a single year. Solomon L. Ginsburg was called a Jewish crusader in Brazil.

He placed high value on the printed page. From his own small funds he bought a press and a few fonts of type to publish a little monthly. The work grew mightily, and when the work of several mission stations was united and taken to Rio de Janeiro, he was chosen to head the work. The literature went to all parts of Brazil, a lasting monument to his faith, labor, and ability. He trained many converts.

He was called home after thirty-three years of labor for Christ in Brazil. The Southern Baptist Convention of the United States, under which he had labored, spoke of him as "decidedly the greatest all-around missionary of any denomination in Brazil." His work lives yet in the hills, valleys, plains, and churches and hearts throughout Brazil.

Leopold Cohn

On Manhattan Island stands the old headquarters building of the American Board of Missions to the Jews, the largest missionary organization of its kind in the world. The work is the result of the faith and vision of Leopold Cohn, missionary pioneer. He was the messenger of God to the Jews of America in the period beginning with the early nineties of the last century and reaching to this day.

Life began for Leopold Cohn in the little town of Berezna, in the eastern part of Hungary. At seven he suffered the loss of both parents in the same year and was left to shift for himself. In those days he learned to trust God. After his confirmation at thirteen, he determined to become a rabbi. At eighteen he graduated from the Talmudic academy with high scholarship and fine recommendations as a teacher.

After being ordained as a rabbi, he contracted a very happy marriage. In the custom of the time, he went to live in his wife's parental home so he could devote himself to further studies in rabbinical lore.

Through years of study, he had thought long on the problems of the exile of Israel and the hope of his people in the Messiah. He gave himself to earnest prayer and study in the hope of finding the solution. Morning after morning he repeated the words of the Maimonides Creed: "I believe with a perfect faith in the coming of the Messiah, and though He tarry, yet will I wait daily for His coming." His desire for the fulfillment of this promise grew greater with the passing days.

Soon he began to rise in the midnight watches and sit on the ground to mourn the destruction of the Temple and to beseech God to send the Messiah soon. He kept asking himself, "Why does the Messiah tarry? When will He come?" One day he found this statement in the Talmud: "The world will stand 6,000 years. There will be 2,000 years of confusion, 2,000 years under the law, and 2,000 years of the time of the Messiah." The commentators noted that after the second 2,000 years Messiah would come and destroy the wicked. His problem became more difficult now; according to these words, the Messiah should have long since come. But Israel was still in exile. He dared not believe the time for Messiah's coming had passed and Messiah had not come after all. He determined to make a new study of the prophecies; but he did so with fear, for the prophets had been forbidden in this respect. The rabbis said: "Cursed are the bones of him who calculates the time of the end." But with irresistible longing he began the study of Daniel.

When he came to the ninth chapter, the light began to dawn on him. From verse 24 he decided that Messiah's coming should have taken place four to five hundred years after Daniel's time. Now he began to doubt the pronouncements of the Talmud in such matters. He was in a desperate struggle now: should he believe God's clear Word or shut his eyes to the truth?

It was the time of the Feast of Dedication, Chanukah, and according to his custom, he planned on preaching on the meaning of the feast. Hardly realizing it, he allowed some of his doubts about the Talmud to escape his lips. Whispers in the congregation soon became an uproar. Petty persecutions followed, and his life was made miserable and his ministry almost impossible. He had never seen a New Testament, and it had never occurred to him to look for help there. He decided to seek help from a fellow rabbi in a distant town, a man his senior by many years.

Before Cohn had finished the unburdening of his troubled soul, the rabbi began to lash him with his tongue and pour out on him a steady stream of insult. He declared that Cohn reminded him of those who claim that the Messiah has already come. He warned him that he would ultimately wind up in disgrace among the apostates in America if he did not cease from his ways.

Disappointed and crushed, Rabbi Cohn left the man he had so respected formerly. But a new idea began to form in his mind. America! The land of freedom! There he would continue his studies. March of 1892 found Rabbi Cohn in the city of New York, warmly welcomed among his countrymen who had known him in Hungary.

One Saturday soon after his arrival, he went out for the customary Sabbath afternoon stroll. He was meditating on the subject of the Messiah. As he was passing by a church located on one of the ghetto streets, his attention was attracted to a sign written in Hebrew, "Meetings for Jews." He thought it strange—a church with a cross on it, and yet a meeting for Jews. A passing friend warned him that in that church were apostate Jews who taught that the Messiah had already come. He wondered if they were the ones spoken of by the rabbi in Hungary.

When he felt he would not be seen, he made his way back to the church. He was dumbfounded to see the speaker on the platform as well as the congregation, bareheaded. This was the height of sacrilege. On the way out he thought he ought to register his protest with the custodian and tell him why he was leaving. He was told he would be welcome to a private interview with the minister at his home.

The next Monday Cohn went to the minister's address. He was impressed with the fact that the minister was a Christian Jew, a learned Talmudist, and a descendant of a rabbinical family. He explained his quest for the Messiah. At the end of the interview, the minister, seeing that Cohn was entirely unaware of the contents of the New Testament, gave him a Hebrew copy of the New Testament.

When Cohn's eyes fell on the first verse, his reaction beggared description. He felt all his trials and separations were soon to receive their reward. He ran as fast as he could to his room, locked the door, and began the study. He began at 11:00 A.M. and ended at 1:00 A.M. He did not understand all, but he could see that the Messiah had come at just the time foretold by Daniel. His joy was boundless.

When he tried the next morning to share his discovery with a rabbi friend, he was rudely shocked. The rabbi snatched the New Testament from his hands, declared it was the product of the apostates, that the Messiah it spoke of was Jesus of the Gentiles, and then threw the book to the ground and trampled it under foot.

Cohn wondered if the Messiah of Israel was the Jesus whom the Gentiles worshiped. To believe in Jesus would be idolatry. He began to study the Bible anew. The picture of the suffering Messiah in Isaiah 53 now gripped him. What if Jesus and the Messiah were the same Person? Could he love the One so hated before? He prayed and fasted. His eyes fell on Malachi 3, and he concluded that Messiah had already come. He fell down and worshiped and determined to serve the Redeemer no matter the cost. Joy filled his soul, and he became a new creature in the Messiah.

He began to preach that Jesus is the Messiah of Israel. His friends were amused and said he was mentally confused because of the long separation from his family. Soon they branded him a traitor and began to persecute him bitterly. When his countrymen wrote his wife of his apostasy, all his correspondence with his family was stopped. The Jews of New York were so aroused that his life was in danger. Some thought it would be a pious deed to remove him from the world.

Friends in his new faith made arrangements, and he was secretly helped to flee to Scotland. In Edinburgh he lived and studied among friends. When the time came for his baptism, gloomy forebodings beset him. He knew it meant the cutting off with all things dear to him before—position, family, friends, all. Dr. Andrew A. Bonar wrote to him: "My people and I were praying for you at our service this morning." He was strengthened through the prayers of God's people.

In time God reunited him with his family, and they too embraced the faith that was his. In 1893 he returned to New York with his family. His one passion now was to preach the Messiah to his brethren. He opened a little mission in the Brownsville section of Brooklyn. The Jews opposed him, and Christians were slow in rallying to him. His wife's jewelry was sold to pay the mission rent. The children were sent to school half-fed. In the course of his ministry, he suffered physical persecution, the marks of which he carried to his death. But God honored the Word and gave him trophies of grace.

He died in 1937, but even in his lifetime he saw the work so humbly begun in the last century reach out to girdle the globe. The servant of God is gone, but the work lives on to this hour. What a contribution to the spiritual life of America!

Samuel Isaac Joseph Schereschewsky

The account would be woefully incomplete without the story of our last personality. It is almost an incredible recital. The door to China was opened in 1858 through treaties with the Western nations. This allowed missionaries to enter the empire and tolerated their religion. In 1831, twenty-seven years before these treaties, Samuel Isaac Joseph Schereschewsky was born to Jewish parents in Tauroggen, Russian Lithuania. He was later called the apostle to China. His native town had some five thousand inhabitants. Both parents died while he was a small boy, so he was cared for by an older brother who was a timber merchant.

Since he was an apt pupil, he was given a good rabbinical training in view of future rabbinical service. Though he later mastered many languages, he always knew Hebrew best. He supported himself while studying at the university at Breslau in Germany.

His first contact with the Gospel came while he was still a student in Lithuania. A fellow student had received a Hebrew New Testament from the London Society for Promoting Christianity among the Jews. He was disinterested in the matter, and gave the book to Schereschewsky. Schereschewsky became convinced that Jesus was the Messiah of the Old Testament predictions. He came under the influence of Dr. S. Neumann, a Jewish Christian missionary of the London Society and lecturer in Hebrew (1834-59) at the University of Breslau. In 1854, when he came to Hamburg to embark for America, he met a Jewish believer who gave him a letter of introduction to the Reverend John Neander, a Jewish Christian pastor of a Presbyterian church in Brooklyn and a missionary to the Jews in New York City. Though Schereschewsky associated with a number of Jewish believers, he was only intellectually convinced of the Messianic faith.

In the spring of 1855, a group of Christian Jews with whom Schereschewsky associated asked him to celebrate the Feast of Passover with them. The Passover meal was eaten with the usual Jewish ceremonies, but at the end, each one stood and told what faith in Jesus the Messiah meant to him. Schereschewsky was deeply and visibly moved. His lips moved in silent prayer. When he arose, his voice was full of emotion as he said, "I can no longer deny my Lord. I will follow Him without the camp." He was baptized shortly after this, and within a year he went to study for the ministry at the Western Theological Seminary in Pittsburgh, Pennsylvania, in 1855. After two years there, he completed his training at the General Theological Seminary (Episcopal) in New York.

In 1859 he applied to the Board of Foreign Missions of the Episcopal Church to go to China. On May 3, 1859 he was accepted. His aim was to go to China to translate the Bible into Chinese.

He sailed on July 13, 1859, with a company of missionaries, for China on the ship *Golden Rule*. The candidates began their study of Chinese on the ship. The trip took almost six months, and it is said that when Schereschewsky landed, he amazed Chinese teachers by his ability to write good, classical Chinese. In Shanghai he gave himself to language study with such industry that once he did not leave the same building for a week. He learned three Chinese languages: Shanghai colloquial; Mandarin; and Wenli, the literary language. By January 1861 he was translating the Psalms into the Shanghai colloquial. The same year, he had reached the western borders of China in his missionary travels, the first Protestant missionary to do so.

From 1861 to 1865 our country was in the agony of the Civil War, and funds from America to China ceased for three years. During this time Schereschewsky acted as Chinese Secretary to the U.S. Legation in Peking and learned the Peking dialect. He also preached regularly. While there, he wrote in 1864: "I am . . . engaged in translating the whole Old Testament into the Mandarin," a language "spoken by more human beings than any other language in the world."

By 1868 he was almost wholly giving himself (except for Sunday preaching) to translation work, using two Chinese copyists. Besides the Old Testament, he translated certain books of the New Testament into Mandarin. The rest was in the hands of other members of the translation committee. It was all finished in September 1872. It marked an epoch in the history of the Bible in China. The American and British Bible Societies published editions of this Bible.

Sixteen years after the translation was completed, a prominent missionary to China wrote: "The translation of the Old Testament into the Mandarin was made by a master hand, seemingly raised up by God for this purpose." No man of his day could equal him in idiomatic use of spoken Mandarin. In 1903 the representative of the American Bible Society in China wrote: "No one not a missionary to China can understand what this work meant and will mean through all time to the Church of Christ in that land. It gave a new impetus to all forms of missionary work and enabled the Churches of all denominations in Mandarin speaking China, so recently opened to them, to train an efficient native ministry and raise up an intelligent church."

Missionaries in China were suggesting in 1874 that Schereschewsky translate the Bible into Mongolian. In 1870, after ten years in China without rest, his health had begun to fail. But he did not want to leave China until the translation work was finished.

In 1875 the family left Peking for furlough and arrived in San Francisco July 1 of the same year. Schereschewsky was admitted to American citizenship in Pittsburgh also in 1875. At home he was praised as the one who made the Bible speak to "nearly half a hemisphere." In 1875 he was elected Bishop of Shanghai but declined. The next year he was elected again and persuaded to accept. In the fall of 1879 he had founded a missionary college, St. John's University, in Shanghai.

In 1878 the Schereschewsky family left for China by way of London to attend the Lambeth Conference of all Episcopal groups. There the Archbishop of Canterbury was reported to have said, "The Bishop of Shanghai is one of six really learned men in the world." Max Muller, the great linguist, said in 1888 that Schereschewsky was "one of the six most learned Orientalists in the world."

Schereschewsky spoke thirteen languages, read twenty, and had at his command between nine and ten thousand Chinese characters. He had begun as an orphan boy and a glazier (for that is the meaning of his surname). The Lord had brought him far.

By October 1878 he was back in Shanghai. While in his duties as Bishop of Wuchang, an unusual hot spell hit Shanghai. On August 12, 1881, he suffered sunstroke. He at once lost almost entirely the use of his limbs. From the beginning his speech was very impaired, but on his lips often were the words, "I must live to revise my translation of the Old Testament." Two weeks after his stroke he said he felt as if he were buried already. All the medical authorities who had been consulted agreed that Schereschewsky had a serious lesion at the base of the brain. Their verdict was that he would never be able to do much work again. He was taken to a famous doctor, Charcot of Paris, who recommended a water cure, which Schereschewsky took in Geneva.

He improved a little but was never able to walk again; he had to be carried the rest of his life. His speech was so blurred that it was hard to understand him. The muscles of his body began to shrink; only his mind came back unimpaired. He stayed in Geneva about four years. In 1886 he planned to return to America, settle in California, and continue his translation work with the help of a Chinese scribe. When he found no suitable Chinese scribe available in California, he asked to be sent back to China.

The American Bible Society was not encouraging, and his church board was not certain. While matters were waiting, he began to use a typewriter he had bought in Switzerland. He found he could type with one finger, the middle finger of his right hand. When his finger refused to serve him, he would take a small stick in his fist and punch the keys with that. In the summer of 1887 he started on one of the most amazing literary undertakings of all time. He began with the revision of the Mandarin Old Testament, hammering with one finger (which soon had a callous on the tip) the English equivalents of the Chinese characters. At first he worked five or six hours a day, then eight and sometimes nine.

In a little over a year the revision was done. Then he went on to translate the entire Bible from the original languages into the easy Wenli, or the current form of the book language of China. Six years were spent on the first draft of the easy Wenli Bible. "I regard it as the most important work of my missionary career," he said. The easy Wenli could be understood by the literate throughout China. Wenli was also used in Korea, Cochin-China, Anam, Tongking, and somewhat in Japan. It was the language of literature among one-fourth of the human race.

He appealed to his board to send him back to China to change the Romanized text into Chinese characters and finish his work. He was sent back at last in 1895. The American Bible Society published it in 1902. The demand was so great that the entire edition was sold out before it came from the press.

When Schereschewsky died on October 16, 1906, he had also completed reference Bibles in Mandarin and easy Wenli.

In characterizing Schereschewsky's final work, Arthur Lloyd, president of Saint Paul's College in Tokyo, wrote: "I very much doubt whether the world has seen any other instance of so great a work accomplished under so great difficulties."

Has Hebrew Christianity made any contribution to America? Let the record speak for itself. It is loud and clear. Praise God!

6

AMERICA'S DEBT TO THE JEWISH HERITAGE

Charles L. Feinberg

It is not uncommon for the uninformed to ask, "What have the Jews ever done for America?" When the subject is carefully searched out, magnitude of the debt that America owes to the Jews staggers the imagination. He who cannot be impressed with the recital of this truth is indeed impervious to evidence and logic.

The Discovery of America

First of all, the Jews played an indispensable part in the discovery of America. The history of the Jews in America starts with the journey of Columbus to America. In Columbus's fleet there were a Jewish interpreter, Luis de Torres; a Jewish surgeon, Marco; and a Jewish physician, Bernal. Another Jew, Rodrigo de Triana, was the first to catch a glimpse of the new land, and the interpreter de Torres was the first white man to tread the soil of America on what came to be known as San Salvador.

But Jews did more than accompany Columbus on his voyage to the west; they played a leading part in making the voyage possible in several ways.[1]

Columbus had strong and influential Jewish friends in the royal court of Spain. They were Louis de Santangel, chancellor of the royal household; Gabriel Sanches, chief treasurer of Aragon; and Cuan Cabrero, the king's chamberlain. These people finally convinced King Ferdinand and Queen Isabella of the importance of the proposed expedition. Santangel personally lent the court 17,000 florins to pay for outfitting the three ships.

The Jews were among the best mapmakers and astronomers in Portugal and Spain, and they helped to provide Columbus with tools of navigation. The sea-quadrant, commonly credited to Regiomontanus, was invented by Levi ben Gerson. Jehuda Cresquea drew the map that Columbus's navigator used. The success of the journey was attributed to Abraham ibn Ezra's knowledge and work in astronomy and navigation. Abraham ben Samuel Zacuto, the most famous mapmaker in Spain, who was also attached to the royal court, made the astronomical tables that guided Columbus through unknown seas.

Yet in 1492 the Spanish monarchs ordered their 300,000 Jewish subjects either to adopt Christianity or leave the country. Most chose exile. Within five years Portugal expelled them as well. Since then neither nation has been a major power in the world.

The American Colonies

Jews were among the earliest settlers in South, Central, and North America. The first English colony in North America was in Jamestown, Virginia, in 1607. The Pilgrims came to Massachusetts in 1620, and in 1654, the first Jewish settlers arrived. They came to New Amsterdam, begun by the Dutch, from the Jewish settlement in Recife, Brazil. When Dutch rule of Brazil passed to Portugal, Jews emigrated to North America for freedom of religion and a better life. In New Amsterdam (New York) they led the struggle for the rights of citizenship and freedom of religion.

Rhode Island, under Roger Williams, was the first colony

in North America to be free from religious persecution. Jews settled there from Holland, Portugal, Poland, Spain, and nearby New Amsterdam, Aaron Lopez came from Portugal and settled in Newport, Rhode Island, and became the chief shipping merchant on the eastern seaboard. At one time he had as many as thirty ships carrying his goods around the world and to the coast cities of the colonies at home.[2] At the beginning of our nation in 1776, of the four million who lived in the thirteen colonies, there were about twenty-five hundred Jews.

Jews joined in the movement westward across our land when large new areas were added to the United States. They aided in the building of towns and opened trade routes to develop business. Some labored as carpenters and iron workers; others were craftsmen and artisans. A number entered politics. Writers found successful careers in journalism, playwriting, and poetry. All in all, they were among the pioneering Americans who grew with the nation.[3]

Revolutionary War

One estimate puts the Jewish population of all the colonies on the eve of the American Revolution at about one thousand. (We have seen that another figure is twenty-five hundred.) The general population of non-Jews totaled over 2.5 million.

The first Jew to die in the War of Independence was Francis Salvador, whose ancestry could be traced back to the Portuguese Marranos (Hebrew Christians). He is buried in South Carolina.

When the British took Savannah in 1778, they placed Mordecai Sheftall, a Jew born in Georgia, on a prison ship. He was the leader of the revolutionary committee of Georgia and a member of the Georgia Brigade, whose duties covered arms and food supply. The British were never successful in getting Sheftall to divulge where the Americans kept their supplies. He finally escaped to Philadelphia. At the conclusion of the war, this patriot was given a land grant for his outstanding service.

Benjamin Nones, a Jew born in France, enlisted in the colonial army as a private and advanced to the rank of major and staff officer. His famous commander, General Pulaski, gave him a citation for "the bravery and courage which a military man is expected to show for the liberties of his country."[4] When the government desperately needed money for the war, Jews played a vital role in financing the Revolution. Some, like Isaac Moses, of Philadelphia, and Jacob Hart, Sr., of Baltimore, made personal loans to the government. Others supplied uniforms, blankets, rifles, and gunpowder. Ship owners turned their ships into raiding vessels to fight the enemy on the high seas; they ran an armed blockade against British merchandise and sank British ships.

The one who did more than any other individual to obtain urgently needed funds for the government to carry on the War of Independence was Haym Salomon, an immigrant from Poland. Salomon landed in New York in 1772. He joined the Sons of Liberty, a group which vigorously promoted the Revolution. When the British took New York, he was arrested as a spy.

When he was freed, he aided French and American prisoners of war to escape. He was able to convince Hessian mercenaries to defect from the British forces. When the British were about to arrest him again, Salomon fled to Philadelphia. Though he arrived in the city penniless, he began to raise money for the revolutionary forces as a broker. It has been estimated that Haym Salomon raised $200,000 to help finance the war. He became known as the "Broker to the Office of Finance" of the United States.[5]

When he died at forty-four years of age, he left a wife and four children, the oldest only seven years old. His widow went to New York from Philadelphia to be supported by relatives.

When it was certain that General Washington would have

to leave New York for a time, Rabbi Gershom Mendez Seixas exhorted his congregation to leave the city with Washington. He argued that to stay would amount to giving support to the British. As a result of his urging most of the congregation left with their rabbi in 1776. It was only in 1783, when the Continental army expelled the British from New York, that they were able to return to their homes.

Article VI of the federal Constitution in 1787, and the First Amendment to the Constitution, both guaranteeing freedom of religion, were considered ample payment for their many sacrifices.

As an interesting postscript, Rabbi Gershom Mendez Seixas, a trustee of King's College (later Columbia University) from 1787 to 1815, was one of the ministers who took part in President Washington's inauguration.

Jewish Names in American Military History

When the United States went to war with Britain in 1812, again the Jews came to the defense of our country. Benjamin Nones, a veteran of the Revolutionary War, fought in the War of 1812. So did a son of Haym Salomon and grandsons of Mordecai Sheftall, as well as several Jewish naval officers. The outstanding Jewish officer in the War of 1812 was Uriah Phillips Levy, who later rose to the rank of commodore. He worked to outlaw flogging of seamen, an effort which was successful in 1862, when Congress outlawed flogging. With some of his funds, he bought and repaired the home of his hero, Thomas Jefferson, at Monticello, Virginia. He and his family requested that it be designated as a national shrine. He gave the government a statue of Jefferson, whom he esteemed as a great liberal and fighter for freedom.[6]

Many Jews fought in the antislavery movement, notably Rabbi David Einhorn (1809-1879), who had to flee from Baltimore because of his fiery sermons. During the Civil War, most Jews of the north and west supported President Lincoln.

Many distinguished themselves in battle. Seven were awarded the Congressional Medal of Honor, our highest military decoration.

Jews, many of whom were newly immigrated from the German States, fought with the army of Texas at the Alamo and in the Mexican War. In the Mexican War, David Camden de Leon served as physician and soldier, winning the distinction of "the fighting doctor."

The Influence of Jewish Law

President Woodrow Wilson, in his treatise on the state, declared:

> It would be a mistake, however, to ascribe to Roman legal conceptions an undivided sway over the development of law and institutions during the Middle Ages. The Teuton came under the influence, not of Rome only, but also of Christianity; and through the Church there entered into Europe a potent leaven of Judaic thought. The laws of Moses as well as the laws of Rome contributed suggestion and impulse to the men and institutions which were to prepare the modern world; and if we could but have the eyes to see the subtle elements of thought which constitute the gross substance of our present habit, both as regards the sphere of private life, and as regards the action of the state, we should easily discover how very much besides religion we owe to the Jew.[7]

Even in times of expulsion of the Jews from a given country, their legal institutions were left behind and appropriated by their enemies. No method has been devised whereby theological, philosophical, political, and economic concepts can be admitted but legal ideas excluded. For example, the "common ancestry of mankind" is an anthropological concept; the so-called brotherhood of man is posited as the same idea in religious terms; the dictum "all men are born equal" is a portion of political philosophy that says the same thing; and "equality before the law" is the legal aspect of the same teaching.

It has long been held that the Western world welcomed Roman law, but in many respects they departed from Roman precedents in the areas of family law, including marriage, divorce, domestic relations, and inheritance. Even in countries influenced by Roman law, it is easier to find a kinship with Judaism than with the civilization of the Roman world. Several attempts in the history of Western civilization to copy the laws of Israel may easily be pointed out: the Code of Alfred the Great of England, Calvin's theocratic state in Switzerland, the laws of Puritan England, and law in America. Anglo-Saxon laws quote the books of Moses, Kings, Job, Psalms, Proverbs, the Apocrypha, and the New Testament books. It was in American colonial times that the judges of Massachusetts, Connecticut, the New Haven colony, and West New Jersey had been charged to inflict penalties according to the "Law of God."[8]

In Pennsylvania at one time, the eldest son inherited a double portion. The isolation of lepers based on Jewish law was cited in a case in Michigan. Quarantine laws were enacted to prevent the spread of disease. The concern evident in Jewish law for the stranger, the afflicted, the widow and orphan, the laborer in the vineyards, the hired man awaiting reward, and the poor debtor, and the laws, its humanitarian measures concerning the ox that treads the corn and the mother-bird—all this has impelled as well as aided and comforted reformers even when their proposed legislation contained none of the terminology of the Bible.[9]

Jewish influence can be seen in the general theory of law that developed in Judea in the time of the birth of Christianity. The Jews developed what is known as *ius naturale et gentium*. They called it the "Seven Commandments for the Descendants of Noah." They held that righteous Gentiles who obeyed these commandments would share in the world to come. Specifically, they were justice between man and man, and prohibition of idolatry, blasphemy, incest, murder, theft, and eating parts cut from living animals. The laws in Leviticus against marriage within forbidden degrees—consanguinity and affinity—found their way into secular systems throughout the Western world.

Returning to the influence of the law of nature, "No other single force has been so potent in the shaping of modern European law as the notion that there was a discoverable law of nature in the universe."[10] Grotius made it the foundation of international law. In the American colonies it furnished the Bill of Rights in the various constitutions. Indeed, the appeal of the Declaration of Independence is to the laws of nature and nature's God. The principle of law as a means of protecting the individual against the power and tyranny of the state, and a recognition of the place of the church in and alongside the state, are traceable to the biblical dictum that there is to be no respect of persons, whether they are influential or not, in judgment.

As for the area of government, the earliest constitutions of the New England colonies were expressly framed after the model of the Mosaic code. Dr. Jonathan Mayhew, who was called "the father of civil and religious liberty in Massachusetts and in America," preached a sermon characterized as "The morning gun of the Revolution." Later in Boston (on May 23, 1766) he said:

> God gave Israel a king (or absolute monarchy) in his anger, because they had not sense and virtue enough to like a free commonwealth, and to have himself for their king,—where the spirit of the Lord is there is liberty,—and if any miserable people on the continent or isles of Europe be driven in their extremity to seek a safe retreat from slavery in some far-distant clime, oh, let them find one in America.[11]

Dr. Samuel Langdon, President of Harvard College and a

recognized authority on the science of government as well as a foremost minister, said:

> The Jewish government, according to the original constitution which was divinely established, if considered merely in a civil view, was a perfect republic. And let them who cry up the divine right of kings consider, that the form of government which had a proper claim to a divine establishment was so far from including the idea of a king that it was a high crime for Israel to ask to be in this respect like other nations, and when they were thus gratified, it was rather as a just punishment for their folly.[12]

Economic Development

The Jews helped significantly in the realm of economics during the transition from a barter economy to a money economy in Europe from AD 1100 to 1350. Moreover, they were part of the transition from a money economy to a credit economy, the present stage of economic development. The modern credit system, and thus modern capitalism, arose from the need of money payments to mercenary soldiers in the wars between Charles V and Francis I, beginning in 1520.

In the sixteenth century, Marranos (converted Jews) spread throughout the New World, forming a financial link between Amsterdam (especially in the seventeenth century) and Mexico, Brazil, Lisbon, Canary Islands, Hamburg, and even London. They were active in bullion brokerage, colonial trade in sugar and indigo. Cromwell used their services in England. Jewish communal development owed much to their wanderings and dispersed family relations. They were pioneers in the field of international finance. Historians of commerce trace the beginning of real joint-stock trading, where shares had a face value endorsed to bearer and could be dealt with as negotiable property, to the forming of the Dutch East India Company, in the first issues of which Jews had a share.[13]

Jewish finance influenced the beginnings of railways in

Europe and America (in our country by Kuhn, Loeb & Company). It was Abraham de Lyon who introduced viticulture in Georgia, where also Dr. Nunes largely developed the growth of indigo.

In California, Jewish firms had much to do with the early economic development, especially in California's connection with Alaska and the seal fisheries which were largely developed by Jewish companies.[14] Copper mining and smelting in America owe much to the firms of Guggenheim and Lewisohn. Jews still predominate in department stores and the clothing industries.

Jewish Contributions in Science, Thought, and Culture

When we consider the spheres of science, thought, and culture, the role of the Jews is central. In the twelfth and thirteenth centuries, Jews in Moslem lands were the intermediaries between the East and West in Greek astronomy, medicine, and especially philosophy (the chief works of Aristotle). They were the catalytic influence in the development of European thought and culture.

It is admitted that the chief influence of medieval Jews on the civilization of Christendom was through their dominant thinkers, Ibn Gabirol and Maimonides. Both were quoted by name and with respect by all the chief scholastics of the thirteenth century: Alexander of Hales (d.1245); Albertus Magnus, count of Bollstädt (1193-1280); and Thomas Aquinas (1225-70). The greatest contribution of Jewish philosophy to modern European thought came through Moses Maimonides (1135-1204). The background of modern scientific ideology is to be found not in the empirical monism of Greece but from the transcendental monotheism of Israel. The concept of absolute cosmic regularity, insofar as it has touched general thought, is of theological origin.[15]

Among eminent Jewish scientists are Harold Urey (b.1893),

who won the Nobel prize in chemistry; Albert Nichelson, and Isidor Rabi (b.1898), who won the Nobel prize in physics; and probably the greatest of them all, Albert Einstein (1879-1955), who developed the theory of relativity, for which he was granted the Nobel prize in 1921. He was a refugee from Nazi Germany.

Adolph Ochs (1858-1935) developed the *New York Times* into one of the world's most influential newspapers. David Sarnoff (1891-1971) rose from messenger boy and wireless operator to become head of the prestigious Radio Corporation of America. Among philanthropists have been Nathan Strauss, Julius Rosenwald (1862-1932), Jacob Schiff (1847-1920), and Felix Warburg (1871-1937).

Supreme Court Justices have been Benjamin Cardozo, (1870-1938); Felix Frankfurter (1882-1965); and Louis D. Brandeis (1856-1941), who said: "American ideals have been Jewish ideals for twenty centuries."[16] There are Jewish judges on every level across the country.

Among noted Jewish physicians are Dr. Joseph Goldberger (1874-1929), who discovered the cause and cure of pellagra; Dr. Casimir Funk (1884-1967), the discoverer of vitamins; Dr. Bela Schick (1877-1967), the developer of the test for diphtheria; Dr. Selman Waksman (b.1888), Nobel prize winner for work in antibiotics; and Dr. Jonas Salk (b.1914) and Dr. Albert Sabin, developers of vaccines against polio.

Jews have contributed to art, music, and the theater. They have enriched the national cultural life as sculptors, artists, composers, singers, instrumentalists (Artur Rubenstein, for one), and conductors. A high percentage of great pianists and violinists are Jews. In the theater they have afforded playwrights, actors, producers, critics, and comedians. They started the movies in 1920.

Many congressmen and senators were Jews—Simon Guggenheim (1867-1941), Benjamin Jonas, Herbert Lehman (1878-1963), and Jacob Javits. Jews have also been governors of some states. They have been presidential advisors, cabinet members, and ambassadors. There are a number of outstanding Jewish novelists. Jewish athletes have engaged in boxing, baseball, basketball, and football.

In education the Hebrew elementary schools and high schools; the Yeshiva University, with its college for women; Einstein Medical College; Isaac Elchanan Theological Seminary; Jewish Theological Seminary of America; Hebrew Union College (in Cincinnati, New York, Los Angeles, and Jerusalem, Israel) ; and Brandeis University, have been in the front ranks.

The Bible: A Gift from the Jews

Far outshining all other contributions of the Jews, and not to be compared in the least with them, is the gift of the Bible, the Scriptures of both the Old and New Testaments. The apostle Paul asked two penetrating questions and followed with two resounding answers in Romans 3:1-2 (NASB): "Then what advantage has the Jew? Or what is the benefit of circumcision? Great in every respect. First of all, that they were entrusted with the oracles of God." If the influence of the Bible was powerful in Old England, it was even more so in New England in the seventeenth century.

The Bible has entered largely into the language of nations. Apart from its heroes—Adam, Noah, Abraham, Joseph, Moses, David, Solomon, Daniel, and the others—the Bible entered into the very speech of everyday life. Notice it in the expressions: "a land flowing with milk and honey"; "a still, small voice"; " a tale that is told"; "by the skin of the teeth"; "lick the dust"; "darkness which may be felt"; "vanity of vanities"; "the law of the Medes and Persians"; "the apple of one's eye"; "eat, drink, and be merry"; "take sweet counsel together"; "grind the faces of the poor"; "cause the widow's heart to sing for joy"; "make a covenant with death"; "heap coals of fire"; "be weighed in the balances and found wanting"; "go to the ant, thou sluggard"; "answer a fool according to his folly"; "a wise son maketh a glad father"; "be not righteous overmuch"; "a soft answer turneth away wrath"; "the race is not to the swift"; "love is strong as death"; "in the multitude of counselors there is safety"; "righteousness exalteth a nation."

As literature, the Bible has no peer, and nothing written can compare with it (even apart from the fact that it is an inspired, inerrant revelation from God). Peters has well said:

> It was the Jews who gave us the Book of books, the Rock of Ages, upon which is built the foundations of all wisdom, that treasure-house from which the children of men have been enriched, that inexhaustible fountain from which the wise drink deep draughts of knowledge and inspiration, that great physician to whom all the afflicted go for cure, that minister who ever solaces the sorrowful, comforts the comfortless and gives hope to the hopeless, that epitome of all that is good and great and noble and elevating and hopeful in the world, in a word, that connecting link between God and man—THE BIBLE. All the books of the Bible, both Old and New Testaments, with the possible exception of the Book of Job, were written by Jews. And who can tell how much the poets, philosophers, sages, and thinkers owe to the Bible? Upon the Bible has been upraised the lofty domes of thought, whose beacon lights guide the world and save it from destruction. The Bible gave us a Dante, a Milton, and a Shakespeare, and millions of others who went to its fountain to seek the source of knowledge, so we can say that indirectly all Christian literature owes much to the Jews.[17]

The first book printed in the colonies was the *Bay Psalm Book,* a translation of the Book of Psalms.[18]

To emphasize the literary value of the Bible without discerning its religious influence is to miss the central factor of the entire question. The culmination, crown, and glory of the Bible consist in its unique revelation of monotheism. Nowhere in the history of man has he ever come to this position through his own thinking and striving. It is first, last, and always a disclosure from God Himself. The monotheism of the Bible is an uncompromising one; it is as adamant against polytheism as it is against henotheism, or monolatry. The Bible's monotheism gave Israel an Object of undivided allegiance, without which there could not be a valid idea of God in the world. Theology always reacts on morality; monotheism in the Bible is an ethical one. It is often forgotten that the prohibition of idols in Israel was a strong preventative against the debased associations of the worship of heathen gods. One's concept of God inevitably carries with it as a corollary that He must have similar qualities in His worshipers.

The world owes to the Old Testament the highest standard of sexual morality in the world. The practice of polygamy with its attendant agonies, so prevalent throughout the ancient world and not yet removed from the world today, finds not one sentence of approval or justification from any of the prophets. Rather, the Old Testament stresses loving and lasting faithfulness to the wife married in youth.

Moreover, in the area of ethics, God reveals Himself as concerned in every relationship and activity of life. As a logical conclusion all action must issue a reward for righteousness and a punishment for sin. Although the Old Testament does not speak explicitly of a future life (cf. 1 Pe 1:5ff.), Jesus rightly inferred from its lofty teaching that "He is not the God of the dead, but the God of the living (Mk 12:27).

What would be the result if the debt of Christianity to the Jews were not recognized? There is such an example in history from an early heretic from Christian orthodoxy, Marcion. This writer determined not to acknowledge any indebtedness to Judaism at all. He rejected outright the authority of the Old Testament and everything in the Gospel that appeared to him to depend on the religion of the Jews. When he did this, he lost monotheism and the sense of unity and goal in the world and in the history of mankind.[19]

All Bible believers owe an inestimable debt to Israel, not only for the preparation for the coming of the Messiah and Saviour but for providing a pattern of worship. The practiced worship of American Christians is based undeniably on the utterances of Israel. Without equivocation the highest, warmest language of devotion is to be traced to the Old Testament. In prayer and praise, Israel has taught the world to say: "I will magnify Thee, O God, my King, and I will praise Thy name forever and ever. Every day will I give thanks unto Thee, and I will praise Thy name forever and ever."

When in our hymnology we recognize God to be the Author of liberty, we are expressing sentiments voiced by Emma Lazarus (1849-1887), a Jewish-American poet and essayist, in her sonnet "The New Colossus," inscribed on the base of the Statue of Liberty.

> Not like the brazen giant of Greek fame,
> With conquering limbs astride from land to land;
> Here at our sea-washed, sunset gates shall stand
> A mighty woman with a torch, whose flame
> Is the imprisoned lightning, and her name
> Mother of Exiles. From her beacon-hand
> Glows world-wide welcome; her mild eyes command
> The air-bridged harbor that twin cities frame.
> "Keep, ancient lands, your storied pomp!" cries she
> With silent lips. "Give me your tired, your poor,
> Your huddled masses yearning to breathe free,
> The wretched refuse of your teeming shore,
> Send these, the homeless, tempest-tost to me,
> I lift my lamp beside the golden door!"

Thank God, the imperishable Jewish nation (Jer 30:11) is linked in so many ways with our beloved nation, the United States of America. In receiving into her bosom the exiled, persecuted children of Abraham, our country has received vastly more than she has ever given. It will ever be so (Gen 12:1-3). Peters has well reminded us: "His race is imperishable; republics may rise and fall, nationalities wither and decay, but ever down the stream of time shall sail the barque of Israel until it loses itself in the illimitable vastness of eternity." Yes, God bless America! And He has promised also: "The Lord will give strength unto his people; the Lord will bless his people with peace" (Ps 29:11).

Do it, Lord, for Thy name's sake!

NOTES

1. *See* Yuri Suhl, *An Album of the Jews in America* (New York: Watts, Franklin, 1972).
2. Ibid., pp. 9-12.
3. *See* Deborah Karp, *Heroes of American Jewish History* (New York: Ktav, 1972).
4. Suhl, *An Album of the Jews in America,* p. 18.
5. Ibid., p. 19.
6. Karp, *Heroes of American Jewish History,* pp. 66-68.
7. Cited by Joseph Jacobs, *Jewish Contributions to Civilization* (Philadelphia: Jewish Publ. Soc. of Amer., 1919), pp. 65-66.
8. N. Isaacs, "The Influence of Judaism on Western Law," in *The Legacy of Israel,* ed. Edwin Bevan and C. J. Singer (New York: Oxford, 1927), pp. 377-406.
9. Ibid., p. 383.
10. Ibid., p. 385.
11. Madison C. Peters, *Justice to the Jews,* new & rev. ed. (New York: McClure, 1908), p. 4.
12. Ibid., p. 5.
13. Jacobs, *Jewish Contributions to Civilization,* pp. 227-28.
14. Ibid., p. 244.
15. Issacs, "Influence of Judaism," in *The Legacy of Israel,* pp. 437-41.
16. Karp, *Heroes of American Jewish History,* p. 137.
17. Ibid., pp. 62-63.
18. Ibid., p. 50.
19. *See* F. C. Burkitt, "The Debt of Christianity to Judaism," in *The Legacy of Israel,* ed. Edwin Bevan and C. J. Singer (New York: Oxford, 1927), pp. 79-80.

7

LIBERTY AND FREEDOM IN THE NEW TESTAMENT

Douglas B. MacCorkle

In 1975, Freedom House made a survey which shows that fewer than one in five persons in our world now live in freedom. This late in history, 44.9% of the world's population is not free in its societies, and only 35.3% is partly free.

These stubborn statistics challenge man's knowledge of true freedom.

But the picture is darker. A sample of the American mood at Bicentennial time (Harris Poll, December, 1975) gives evidence that 58% to 37% do not believe that *all* people can enjoy individual freedom.

It appears that freedom is a problem to man. It is a problem in terms of achieving it generally. It is a problem for man to sustain an enjoyment of the relative freedom he may have. The only real light on the scene comes from the revelation of God in His Word. The condition of man has long since challenged God, and He has done something major about it.

The Concept of Freedom

Man has been making footprints on the freedom trail for about seven thousand years. But not one person has ever experienced complete or universal freedom. Oh yes, there have been times of temporary or relative freedom, but nothing universal or permanent. What then is this elusive human idea or ideal?

Crabb's *English Synonyms* makes a distinction which lies deep in the essence of this major but rather abstract idea. Crabb distinguishes liberty from freedom in this manner: (1) liberty is to be understood as the *public* aspect in the idea. That is, the great liberator has won liberty for a nation; (2) freedom is the *private* aspect in the idea. That is, the one for whom liberty has been won publicly can enter in and enjoy the personal freedom resulting from the liberating action as structured in the new constitution or charter.

When we speak of the free world, we deny that freedom is worldwide. We are also talking about the political concept of freedom, as did the Greeks.

Americans are thinking in Bicentennial terms these days. This means that liberty and freedom play a major part in celebrations. In the United States Declaration of Independence is a *public* declaration of life, *liberty,* and the pursuit of happiness that is accentuated in this great document of State. In the Liberty Bell is a *public* declaration that the previous statement has been adopted by our nation. In the Statue of Liberty is a symbol constantly declaring the enjoyment of *liberty* under a free form of government. The American flag is preeminently a symbol of *liberty,* with *liberty* and justice for all. And in "America the Beautiful" we sing,

> O beautiful for pilgrim feet,
> Whose stern impassioned stress,
> A thoroughfare for *freedom* beat,
> Across the wilderness.
> America, America,
> God mend thine every flaw,
> Confirm thy soul in self-control,
> Thy *liberty* in law [italics mine].

But perhaps only the meek see and grasp the transition set

before us in the great hymn which says: "Our Fathers' God, to Thee, Author of liberty, to Thee we sing." Yes! It was He that set up Israel to recognize the structure of liberty, when He inscribed these words in the Old Testament: "You shall thus consecrate the fiftieth year and proclaim a release through the land to all its inhabitants. It shall be a jubilee for you" (Lev 25:10, NASB).

Symbols and Scripture all attempt to make the abstract concrete. What is done at the public and national level is most easily seen. What results in the individual freedoms is more elusive and passing. Thus we must look to a higher court of appeal and reach for the latest word from that source: the New Testament and its teaching concerning liberty and freedom.

The Public Concept of Freedom

In the New Testament, the public aspect of liberty and freedom is eminently connected with the first advent of Jesus as Messiah.

Early in His public, formal, national ministry, the Messiah took the synagogue scroll containing the prophecy of Isaiah and deliberately opened to what we today know as chapter 61. He read verse one and the first clause in verse two.

It was a reading that placed a heavy accent upon His own concept of His ministry and message. It stressed the theme of liberty and freedom. Both ideas were substantial factors in the Gospel He was to preach throughout the land. It was a reading that was made in close proximity to His triumph over the devil's testing in the wilderness, from which He returned "in the power of the Spirit."

> The Spirit of the Lord is upon Me,
> Because He anointed Me to preach the Gospel to the poor
> He has sent Me to proclaim release to the captives,
> And recovery of sight to the blind,

To set free those who are downtrodden,
To proclaim the favorable year of the Lord (Lk 4:18-19, NASB).

He explicitly stated, "Today this Scripture has been fulfilled in your hearing" (Lk 4:21, NASB).

The Messiah's sense of timing and theme were what we can call "world class." He knew the hour as well as the message for the hour. Furthermore, He was promising what He alone could bring to pass: the freeing of His people.

This message was a *national* message. The Messiah did not visit other capitals or other nations. He came to Israel because of the deep dealings with it over a fifteen-hundred-year period. He was operating under the guarantees and sanctions of God (the biblical covenants) given only to that nation (Ro 9:1-4). This is the same nation that He set at liberty from Egypt and from Babylon. This is the nation He has placed in the center of things for the future (Is 2:1-4). It should have been good news to them to know: (1) *the time,* "the acceptable year of the Lord"; "Today is this Scripture fulfilled in your hearing"; (2) *the proclamation,* "release to the captives"; "to set free those who are downtrodden."

This message was a *formal* message. The Messiah was here on His Father's business: (1) "The Spirit of the Lord is upon Me"; He was filled with a Gospel message; (2) "He anointed Me"; He was provided with power for the mission; (3) "He has sent Me"; He was given a specific mission.

This message was a *public* message. The Messiah was publicly introduced to the whole nation for one year (by John the Baptizer, Mt 3:1-12) as the Lord! After John was cast into prison, the Messiah began to preach publicly (Mt 4:12, 17).

Careful exposition of the New Testament requires that we understand that the death of the Messiah was to Israel the death of their King (Mt 2:2, 4; 27:11, 29, 37; Jn 19:21). It was on the battlefield of Calvary that the Messiah won liberty for the captives. In His resurrection, He expected and expects that victory to be enjoyed through the enjoyment of individual freedom along the lines He prescribed in sacred Scripture. The concept of liberty and freedom has indeed gone public. Men are divided pro and con; none has been able to maintain neutrality, and all know the claims. The first advent of Christ and the occasion of His entrance into history made the concept public and so vivid that it remains unabated to this hour.

Once within the human structure of time and circumstances, the Messiah *enunciated* the good news of liberty and freedom.

First of all He pointed out the yoke of religious bondage under which the whole nation was fettered (Mt 11:28-30, NASB). It was the basic bondage, the bondage of the soul. "Come to Me, all who are weary and heavy-laden, and I will give you rest. Take My yoke upon you, and learn from Me, for I am gentle and humble in heart; and YOU SHALL FIND REST FOR YOUR SOULS. For My yoke is easy, and My load is light."

The nations of the world have largely learned that liberty can be enjoyed as freedom for the individual only when it operates within a category of prescribed structure. The world has a major ingredient missing, however, in that it has no person who can catalyze the factors. That person would have to be like our Person, alive in the power of an endless life. The Messiah enunciates matters clearly. It is necessary to bypass all other approaches because they are wearying and burdensome. The only approach to liberty and personal freedom is through the Person of the Messiah.

In a Bicentennial celebration does the Messiah stand taller than William Penn, John Hancock, George Washington, Ben Franklin, or a host of others? Yes, indeed; where they were mere men of like passions, the Messiah has always stood taller and speaks more clearly, even on their favorite subjects of liberty and freedom.

What then is the secret of this enunciation? Is it not the fact that an individual who enjoys the freedom of the Messiah's liberating work and victory does so because he leaves a bondage which he was in unwillingly, for one which he is in willingly? For to take the yoke of the Messiah upon us is to voluntarily seek to enjoy the higher freedom of being the Messiah's bondslave. That is the only way man can find ease instead of weariness, lightness instead of being heavy ladened.

Although there exists a large vocabulary of interacting concepts in the New Testament, we must select the classic proclamation of the Messiah identified in John's gospel, 8:31-36 (NASB):

> Jesus therefore was saying to those Jews who had believed Him, "If you abide in My word, then you are truly disciples of Mine; and you shall know the truth, and *the truth shall make you free.*" They answered Him, "We are Abraham's offspring, and have never yet been enslaved to anyone; how is it that You say, 'You shall become free'?" Jesus answered them, "Truly, truly, I say to you, everyone who commits sin is the slave of sin. And the slave does not remain in the house forever; the son does remain forever. If therefore *the Son shall make you free, you shall be free indeed*" [italics mine].

It was comparatively simple to believe the truth of a miracle performed before the eyes of Messiah's contemporaries. But these truths simply piled up evidence that gave new difficulty to deny or counteract. The Messiah's message was far more penetrating than that. He could spell out His truth definitively, and if a man lived in the illumination and saturation of His Word (truth), that truth would make him free. That truth would bring any man into a freedom to enjoy a new life design or life-style.

But we must understand that this is not cheap freedom to

do whatever we as individuals dream up. Such would be a wild kind of life. It would be a soft or permissive life, a life of license (that is libertarian).

And we must understand that His truth is liberating in that it is the factor He employs within man to effect there what has outwardly been achieved by Him alone at His scene of victory, Calvary. The truth alone cannot set man free. This truth must be employed in the hands of the Liberator, the Messiah. As verse 36 indicates, it is when the Son sets us free that we are free indeed. It is liberating truth—a corpus of truth in itself—in the hands of a liberating Messiah that frees man *from* a multitude of bondages and frees him *to* a completely new context and content of life.

Perhaps a glimpse at a well-told example will engrave this firmly on our hearts. In Genesis 2-3 it is clear that God commanded Adam and Eve to eat the tree of life. This not only freed them to eat but informed them that it was specifically appropriate to do so. It is obvious that neither Adam nor Eve employed or enjoyed this freedom to eat the tree that symbolized eternal life. This *positive* commandment has suffered at the hands of commentators. The first couple actually defaulted on this freedom before they sinned against the negative commandment relating to the tree of the knowledge of good and evil. Adam and Eve were *free* to enjoy positively all that the first tree represented. This is the freedom *to* something more substantial than anything else in the context. So man today is also well informed by God's Word (truth) which God Himself will employ to set man *free to* enjoy all that this Word (truth) calls for.

Men have tried other formulas to religious freedom. They have tried the alleged truths of ritualism. Israel had more than enough of these elements, but they were blind to the bondage of the ritualism they endorsed (Jn 8:33). At the same time, they were blind to the information about Abraham. Before them stood Abraham's chosen and chief Seed, and they did not recognize Him because they did not know the Abrahamic truth nor Abraham's heavenly Father.

Men have tried to achieve through other merit systems also. These systems are all self-serving. They are all do-it-yourself salvation formulas.

At the same time, men have tried to press into the resources of thought to get at the core truth they know must be a secret and must lie beyond the average, natural man's grasp. They have not been set free by methods of concentration and meditation, such as Transcendental Meditation (TM). It is only by meditating on God's Word day and night that a man is blessed with sound freedom, such as John 8 enunciates.

So the Messiah has publicly announced the truth concept of freedom. Mary Baker Eddy thought she and her followers could make it on John 8:32 alone; but it has been publicly stated and demonstrated that only when the Messiah employs the Word of God is man freed indeed (Jn 8:36). In this year when liberty and freedom are everywhere proclaimed, let us remember how clearly and publicly the Messiah proclaimed true freedom, based upon His liberating work.

The Personal Concept of Freedom

The Messiah has been here and gone. On His arrival back home, He sent the third Person of the Trinity—the Holy Spirit—to introduce major transfigurations of systematic truth that would operate on the power generated by His finished work on Calvary's cross.

In time, the Spirit involved selected writers to provide the dimensions of that which Messiah had enunciated in His public, formal, and national earthly ministry. Thus, the basic freedom declared by the Messiah in John 8:31-36 is substantially explained and applied in the Scriptures of the New Testament epistles. This is the script that the Holy Spirit is following during the time when the Messiah is calling forth through Gospel preaching a Bride for His name. Only this script provides the true liberty and freedom the whole world of people has gotten lost seeking. That is why patriotism has to be awakened at Bicentennial time. Liberty was provided in the separation of the United States from England two hundred years ago; but *personal* freedom is not a top number on Americans' enjoyment list. *Personal* freedom comes to one only through the work of liberty performed publicly and alone for every man at the Cross. The classic call to freedom, in all the ages, is not the "Let My people go" of Egypt but the calling of man into the freedom John 8:31-36 speaks about.

To the cries of Matthew 11:28-30 and John 8:31-36 must be added that battle cry of Galatians 5:1. Now, Galatians is Romans with its sleeves rolled up. This lends the idea that Paul is at war at Galatians, reawakening Galatian believers to their calling to *personal* freedom. Galatians has often been called the Magna Carta of freedom. This freedom is not one of many but the only legitimate one.

Hear that cry again: "It was for freedom that *Christ set us free;* therefore keep standing firm and do not be subject again to a yoke of slavery" (Gal 5:1, NASB, italics mine).

Christ could set us *free* because He met all our obligations before God when He emptied the penal cups of sin and death on the cross. It would be a denial of the finished work of the Messiah on the cross to put people under obligation to any favorite or false system of religious activity. It is our responsibility to stand firm in this freedom *from* all other obligations but one: we are obligated to enjoy fully what He provided at the greatest of all prices.

Personal freedom, then, is conceived in the New Testament as being enjoyed under a new system. This system is carefully personalized by the Holy Spirit and administered by Him while the Messiah is in session at God's right hand, where He awaits every enemy being made the footstool under His feet (Heb 1:13).

This freedom (in the New Testament, the same Greek

word is used for both freedom and liberty) is something that must be maintained. Even in Paul's day it was being spied out (Gal 2:4), and we are warned to "keep standing firm" in it (Gal 5:1), because unsaved and enslaved man desires to apply a yoke of slavery or bondage to people Christ has set free.

This freedom increases in stature as we understand it more. Some of the basic freedoms stated in the New Testament floodlight the bondages *from* which born again Christians were freed:

1. Freedom from the bondage of sin (see Jn 8:31-36; Ro 6: 18—7:25) means freedom from the *penalty* of sin, from the *power* of indwelling sin, and from the *presence,* eventually, of sin. Only the Messiah can handle the sin problem in man.
2. Freedom from the bondage of the law (see Ro 7:3-25; 8: 2; Gal 2:4; 3:13; 4:4, 21-31; 5:1, 13) means freedom from the only religious system God ever gave. It was a legal system. It was given to identify sin. It could not justify, sanctify, or glorify a man. It could only slay him (2 Co 3:1-16). The Messiah met all its claims.
3. Freedom from the bondage of self (see Gal 2:20-21) means that the great ego (see 2 Ti 3:2-5) cannot bind us. We are freed from our most intimate and greatest enemy—ourselves. Being free we are indwelled, in that new ego, by the Messiah Himself. This is the genius of successful freedom. Here in Galatians it is written in the biblical Declaration of Dependence (upon the Messiah).
4. Freedom from the bondage of death (see Ro 6:21; 8:21; Heb 2:15) means freedom from man's greatest enemy outside himself, through the action of a substituted legal death on the part of the Messiah. But this freedom can only be enjoyed in the resurrection and resurrection life of the Messiah.

It is this freedom that caused Paul to confront Peter (Gal

2) so that the truth of the Gospel might continue to us. As Romans 8:2 shouts to us in the midst of the greatest of all New Testament jubilee passages: "For the life-giving principles of the Spirit have *freed you in Christ Jesus* from the control of the principles of sin and death" (Berkeley version, italics mine). Chapter eight of Romans systematically sets forth the jubilee climate in which the free life in Christ operates satisfyingly and successfully. Paul admitted he *enjoyed* this freedom in Christ. He also said, "Where the Spirit of the Lord is, there is *liberty*" (2 Co 3:17*b*, NASB).

At this time in which the Church finds itself in the age and world, the ages have not developed to their predicted fullness. Thus there is still the tension natural to freedom. Galatians 5:13 (NASB) says, "For you were called to freedom, brethren, only do not turn your freedom into an opportunity for the flesh." Our freedom was never intended to be a springboard for license. It was intended to be employed to enter into a positive enjoyment of all that the liberating work of Christ on the cross opened to all believers. Does the Messiah have the right answer to this tension? Certainly!

The greatest key in all the Bible is found three verses away, at Galatians 5:16-17 (NASB): "But I say walk, by the Spirit, and you will not carry out the desire of the flesh. For the flesh sets its desire against the Spirit, and the Spirit against the flesh; for these are in opposition to one another, *so that you may not do the things that you please*" (italics mine). The Spirit is deliberately set to oppose the desires of our flesh so that the result may be assured, namely, that *we will not do our own will.* This is an inside action. This will bring the believer into a higher freedom, a positive freedom, the freedom that God Himself enjoys.

All of this is assisted by a valuable spin-off from the Messiah's words of John 8:32, "Ye shall know the truth and the truth shall set you free." That falls off the pen of James (1:25 and 2:12, NASB) in the following instructive ways: "But one who looks intently at the perfect law, the law of liberty, and abides by it, not having become a forgetful hearer but an effectual doer, this man shall be blessed in what he does.

"So speak and so act, as those who are to be judged by the law of liberty."

The Word of God, our Bible, is the perfect law of liberty. It shows us what pleases God and what is His will. Within this will, freedom works to perfection for every born again child of God. The Word keeps him clear mentally and vigorous spiritually. It is a perfect New Testament law and order for freedom and freed living.

Finally, the personal concept of freedom contains another check, another balancing factor. This factor is the truth that we are now *bondservants* to Another. As Matthew 11:28-30 previously indicated, we are to take His yoke upon us and learn from Him, for His yoke is easy and His burden is light. The apostle Paul spells this out in Romans 6:18, 20, and 22: "Having been freed from sin, you were made slaves of righteousness. . . . For when you were slaves of sin, you were freed in regard to righteousness. . . . But now having been freed from sin and enslaved to God, you derive your benefit, resulting in sanctification, and the outcome, eternal life" (NASB).

In effect, we have been transferred into the realm of the Messiah in advance of His earthly millennial reign (Col 1:13). The Messiah's task now is to fill the role of Master and turn out masterpieces. We are *free* to have this privilege of being a masterpiece in process. God is *free* to conform us to the image of His Son. These two aspects of freedom are contemplated in the biblical doctrine of predestination (Ro 8:29).

So, then, when we locate the perfect law of liberty and identify it as the Word of God and look into it intently, then is brought to pass the saying, "But we all, with unveiled face beholding as in a mirror the glory of the Lord, are being transformed into the same image from glory to glory, just as from the Lord, the Spirit" (2 Co 3:18, NASB). This is how God conceives personal freedom in its most prominent aspects.

When the Personal and Public Concepts of Freedom and Liberty Combine

At His first advent, when the Messiah picked up the Isaiah scroll and turned deliberately to chapter 61:1-2*a*, He read only up to a definite point, ending with, "to proclaim the acceptable year of the Lord." Or to state it in the words of another, "to proclaim the year of the Lord's favor." But He stopped short of a clause or two that relate to His anticipated second advent. These clauses read, "And the day of vengeance of our God; to comfort all that mourn." There will be a day of complete adjudication connected with the second advent of the Messiah. Since that day will bring in a permanent and universal peace, it will also combine personal and public liberty and freedom as never before in history. Isaiah 61:3 adds, "To appoint unto those who mourn in Zion, to give unto them beauty for ashes, the oil of joy for mourning, the garment of praise for the spirit of heaviness, that they might be called trees of righteousness, the planting of the Lord, that he might be glorified." The mourning of the seven years prior to His touchdown on the Mount of Olives will need His comfort (Zec 12:10; Mt 5:4; Rev 1:7).

In the days of the first advent, the proclamation of freedom was slanted to one land—Israel. At the second advent, the whole world will be in His purview. This time, the trumpet of jubilee will be blown and the freedom that is beyond all that man has dreamed will come to earth. The Israelites who have been bonded throughout the nations in a God-designed Diaspora will be freed and brought back to their land, which itself will be brought to its covenant boundaries. The Gentile nations will be freed from the devil's world system.

When we recall the statements of Luke 2:38 and 24:21 at

the beginning and close of His first advent, we can understand why they were related to advent all right, but to the second advent. Anna, the prophetess, "continued to speak of Him to all those who were *looking for the redemption of Jerusalem*" (Lk 2:38, NASB). The disciples on the road to Emmaus, "were hoping that it was He who was going to redeem Israel" (Lk 24:21, NASB).

These expectations were not wrong. They were corroborated by His Word and implemented perfectly in His finished work upon the cross. Now the Liberator can return in power and great glory to apply true personal freedom on a universal basis as always by grace and through faith.

8

AMERICA AND BIBLE PROPHECY

Douglas B. MacCorkle

America's geography existed prior to 1492, or Columbus could not have discovered it! The United States of America is involved in Bible prophecy, even if many students have neither discovered nor explored the fact. Perhaps some students shrink from a thorough study of our nation in predictive prophecy.

But America *is* in the world geographically and in the world system politically. Admittedly, it is a late arrival. Discovered about 484 years ago, it has been a duly constituted nation for only 200 years. Could God have foreseen its appearance on the international scene? Could it have been clearly included in His graphic international predictions?

If the whole world currently considers the USA either the number one or two world power; and if the second-advent world crisis is drawing nearer, is it possible that the USA will be isolated from major world events, in which it is clearly stated that the whole world is involved? Let us search and suggest answers from divine Scripture.

The World in Bible Prophecy

The term *cosmos* is translated "world" about one hundred eighty-six times in the New Testament. It plays as large a role as its many occurrences suggest.

But the King James Version of the Bible usually translates

three Greek words "world." Because the English word *world* is relatively general in its meaning, the reader could be unaware of its thrust. It is quite relevant to unravel its meaning in this context.

THE WORLD AS A CREATED PLACE

The geographic aspect of the term *world* is perhaps the first picture man gets. But if we think of this matter prophetically, we can understand why the world came into being. And we can understand that a *prophetic* word spoken by God brought a specific creation out of nothing.

Man was a created being. Before the Fall, man was given dominion, as described in Genesis 1:28-30; Psalm 8:6; and Hebrews 2:6-8. Indeed, man is the primary reason for the creation of the world.

Because of the Fall, man requires rescue by divine salvation. Salvation puts man in a position to have dominion, as provided in God's original mandate. But it is true that "now we see *not yet* all things put under him" (Heb 2:8*b*). What we do see *now* is Jesus (Heb 2:9), who was for a little while made lower than the angels for the suffering of the death of the cross, which in turn renders the world salvable. We see Jesus crowned with glory and honor in the aspect of the second Adam and already seated at the right hand of the Majesty on high (Heb 1:3; 12:1-2). He sits there as the New Man. He has won and will share dominion on schedule (Rev 3:21). His headship on earth at His second advent will bring man into that intended and predicted dominion over the whole world. The world was created for this activity of man, and the original purpose will be actualized, beginning with the Millennium.

THE WORLD AS A CONTESTED SCENE

Four chapters deep into the New Testament, we find the devil making a bona fide offer of the kingdoms of this world to the Messiah (Mt 4:8-9). Note that the devil controls them and has divided them up. The same devil is the god of this age (2 Co 4:3-4), as a usurper.

Now, an age (like our English word *eon*) is a block of action in a period of time. The time element, however, is merely coincidental. It is the *kind* of action that is distinctive. This *kind* of action is labeled the deception of the nations in Revelation 20:1-3. Throughout history several *ages* have run their course through the world scene, a contested scene, because the usurper has so far been visibly effective in delaying the reign of Messiah.

The curtain is lifted in prophecies such as Daniel and the Revelation, so that we can clearly identify the contest in the world scene between the Messiah and the devil. The issue being contested is dominion. Through the Messiah's power, man will have that dominion at the end of the contest, and that dominion will be over this world, of which the United States of America is an integral part. The kingdom of this world will one day be the kingdom of our Lord and Saviour (Rev 11:15).

THE WORLD AS A COMPREHENSIVE SYSTEM

The most helpful definition of the term *world* in New Testament usage is "world system." The whole world system lies in the lap of the wicked one (Satan), according to 1 John 5:19*b*. Whoever is a friend of the world system is at war with God (Ja 4:4).

This world system covers the whole world. It is against its high organization that Christians are to wrestle (Eph 6:12). It was highly organized on a national basis also in Daniel's day (Dan 10:13). The system is *anti-Messiah* at its root, and it will be destroyed forever at His second advent (Rev 19:11-21). Its greatest problem is the act of God in placing Israel in the navel of the earth and in the titling of the land of Palestine to her forever. Herein lies the story of the world system's life.

The World's Nations in Prophecy

If some doubt that the USA could be included in God's predictive prophecies before it was discovered, they should study the case of Israel in terms of the arrangement of nations and their alignments.

ARRANGEMENT OF THE NATIONS BY GOD

We are told in Genesis 10:25 that in the days of Peleg—a descendant of Shem—*the earth was divided.* This occurred after the Flood, of course. (It is cited also in 1 Ch 1:19.) The name Peleg means "division." God is identifying His ordering of the world by dividing the people *embryonically.* From this dividing action will eventuate nations and national boundaries. Genesis 10 treats an earth that had one language and dialect (Gen 11:1) and that was about to build the tower as a symbol of one world. Its location in Babylon was of great and lasting significance (cf. Rev 17-18). Soon, Babylon would also open the times of the nations (Dan 9:24-27).

But this division had as its core the nation that was not to be counted among the nations (Num 23:9). Israel was chosen of God to be a peculiar people unto Himself, *above all the nations that are upon the earth* (Deu 14:2*b*). In fact, Deuteronomy 32:8 cannot be misunderstood: When the Most High divided to the nations their inheritance, when He separated the sons of Adam, He set the bounds of the people according to the number of the children of Israel.

In addition, the land was given in covenant for an everlasting possession (Gen 17:8). Even though Israel shall be dispersed into all nations (Deu 28:63-65), they will be brought back into the land titled to them, by divine power (Deu 30:3-5). Certainly God "hath not dealt thus with any [other] nation" (Ps 147:20*a*). But He has indeed arranged the international scene with the nation Israel at its core.

ALIGNMENT OF THE NATIONS PROPHETICALLY

Years later the southern two tribes were in Babylon as captives of Nebuchadnezzar. In sovereign grace, God gave the conquering king a dream and the conquered prophet, Daniel, a vision (Dan 2 and 7) of the times of the Gentiles. Or we might better call it the times of the nations. These times had a specific beginning with Nebuchadnezzar (Dan 2:38) and ending with the second advent of the Messiah, which is concurrent with the return of Israel to its land in belief (Lk 21: 24-30).

In Daniel 2, God gave a graphic image-profile of the international alignment of nations for what has already amounted to over 2500 years. The approximate relationships of this graphic dream are summarized:

	Daniel 2 Metals	Daniel 7 Beasts	Meaning	Dates in History
1.	2:32, 37, 38 Gold	7:4 Lion/Eagle	Babylon	606-536 BC
2.	2:32, 39 Silver	7:5 Bear/Ribs	Medes-Persians	536-331 BC
3.	2:32 Brass	7:6 Leopard/Heads	Greece	331-146 BC
4.	2:33, 40 Iron	7:7 Nondescript	Rome	146-

It is obvious that a king of kings exists at the start of this structuring (Dan 2:37) and the King of kings at its close (Rev 19:16). Again, there is an obvious deterioration in the value of the metals (i.e., the kingdoms), and an obvious increase in the strength of the same metals, until the toes come into view, and there a composition of weak and strong elements is accented. The glory of gold is not seen in the composition of iron and clay, but it must be observed that the gold, silver, brass, and iron are *all* standing in this structure when the stone destroys the entire image at the same time. This "mix" is both in the whole image and in the toes at the end.

ANTITHESES OF THE NATIONS PROPHESIED

When the ten nations (toes, horns) come together for their purpose (Ps 2; Rev 19:11-21) it will be a curious combination indeed. It will be a mixture of strength and weakness (Dan 2:21-43); and they will not adhere to one another because of major philosophic differences or antitheses.

How they can combine for their purposes is unveiled in Revelation 17:12-14. They find a leader in the Antichrist and are willing to trust him for one hour. So they mentally concur with him and provide him with their power and strength so that they can unite the world in making war on our Messiah. That the Messiah is their common enemy unites strong and weak nations. The timing of it all is determined by the authority of God which supports and surfaces what is found behind the seals, trumpets, and bowls of Revelation chapters 6-19. So whether the forms of their governments are monarchial, republic, democratic, or whatever, they will give up their distinctives to battle the Messiah openly at the end of the alignment prophesied. And if any contemporary today objects, it should be asserted that these alignments can only occur in the closing period structured in Scripture. While we may try to identify *trends* toward these things, we can not see the *ends* that are in view. Nevertheless, in those *ends* we know there will be a mix, and the whole Western world will be in action—including the United States of America.

The World of America in Bible Prophecy

The world in which the USA exists currently is one in which Israelites are still officially dispersed. Israel is not now and will not be brought back officially into its land *in belief* until the Messiah's second advent (Mt 24:31). But, at long last, the power blocs of the world have taken shape in relationship to Palestine's north, south, east, and west.

When reading the Bible, one has to understand that it can be general as well as specific. In the latter case, we have an illustration in Micah 5:2, where it specifically states that the Messiah was to be born in Bethlehem of Ephrathah. In the former case, Acts 1:8 has spoken generally: "Jerusalem, all Judea, and in Samaria, and to the uttermost part of the earth."

It will be demonstrated now that the points of the compass set forth in Daniel 11:40-45 are general. It appears, also, that such factors as ten toes or ten horns (i.e., ten kings or kingdoms) fall into the same general classification. *No one* can possibly identify the ten kingdoms of the alleged Roman Empire revival. Even those who assume they know, place them all *west* of Palestine as a political bloc.

THE WORLD LOOKED AT GEOGRAPHICALLY

In most writings on prophetic themes, the USA usually appears in one of the following ways: (1) as one of the *isles* of Psalm 72:10; (2) as two wings of a great eagle of Revelation 12:14; (3) as Tarshish with all the young lions thereof, of Ezekiel 38:13. All such identifications require a stretch of the allegorization technique.

There has been a major development of all compass points since the days of the Old Testament prophets. Such things never maintain the status quo. And nomenclature also changes in such a development. The size of the world has increased in such matters as population, areas developed, and wealth. Parallel is the fact that Israel was never a *world* body, but the

Church is. A whole world, in outline in the prophets, is now a complete picture.

As we turn to the classic text of Daniel 11:40-45, we are faced with the important time note. We are brought by prophecy to "the time of the end" (11:40). The New Testament (Mt 24:3, 14, and the intermittent sequence of whens and thens in chaps. 24-25) refers to the same "end" or, better, "consummation." When properly correlated (Bible-wide), this end time is generally the Day of the Lord and more specifically the Great Tribulation period closing the current age. The Church is in this present age but not of it (Jn 17:16; Gal 1:4). The secrets of this age are devulged to the disciples of the Messiah in Matthew 13. But the consummation of this age draws our fullest attention because of our subject. For it is specifically in that time-of-the-end context that we are, for the first time, asked to note the four points of the compass as pivoted from Jerusalem or Palestine. The time note governs this context in that sense.

The kings of the North, South, and East are very clearly identified by the Holy Spirit respectively in Daniel 11:40, and 44; Daniel 11:40, 42, and 43; and Daniel 11:44.

Two lines of study will provide substantiation that the pronouns to be listed below all refer to the king of the West who, in this Daniel 11 context, is also the Antichrist (Dan 11:36-39; cf. 2 Th 2:1-10). The first line of study is to identify the preceding context in Daniel 11:1-39 and the succeeding context in Daniel 12. The second line of study is to diagram the English translation of the two contexts and our classic central passage. As you search these verses, you will discover the context to be, in outline, something like this:

I. Specific Prediction of Historical Events Between Syria and Egypt from about 300 BC to about 150 BC, Dan 11: 2-35

   A. Transition from Medo-Persia and Greece, Dan 11:2-

4 (Alexander the Great is the hero-king of v. 3)

B. Alexander the Great's kingdom divided in four segments, Dan 11:4

C. Two of his four generals singled out and described
   1. The Ptolemies, kings of the south, Dan 11:5-9
   2. The Seleucids, kings of the north, Dan 11:5-9
   3. Antiochus the Great, king of the north, battling with the king of the south, Dan 11:10-20
   4. Ptolemy Philopater, king of the south, battling with the king of the north, Dan 11:10-20
   5. Exchange of wins and losses, Dan 11:10-20

D. Antiochus Epiphanes, Dan 11:21-35
   1. His ascent to power in his sectors, Dan 11:21-24
   2. His battles with the king of the south, Dan 11:25-30*a*
   3. His plundering of Israel, Dan 11:30*b*-35

II. Predictive Profile of Antichrist, Dan 11:36-45
   A. His megalomania, Dan 11:36-39
   B. His campaigns, Dan 11:40-45

III. Predictive Period of Antichrist's Operation, Dan 12:1-12
   A. Israel's protection in the period, Dan 12:1
   B. Israel's resurrection at close of the period, Dan 12:2-3
   C. Chronological indications for the period, Dan 12:4-12

Space forbids diagramming this context. A key discovered, however, is that Daniel 11:36-39 shows that the first *him* in verse 40 must refer to its antecedent—the Antichrist of verses 36-39. The second key is to trace the personal pronouns *he* and *him* so that they avoid throwing the king of the north against the king of the north, as is often done unwittingly.

The pronouns referred to appear as follows: Daniel 11:40, *him, him, he;* Daniel 11:41, *he, his;* Daniel 11:42, *he, his;* Daniel 11:43, *he, his;* Daniel 11:44, *him, he;* Daniel 11:45, *he, he, his, him.* It is demonstrable, by diagramming, that this series of pronouns all refer to the Antichrist in the time of the end. It follows that the Antichrist is a Western ruler.

THE WORLD LOOKED AT POLITICALLY

With the foregoing pattern in our minds, we can look at matters politically "at the time of the end."

The Antichrist is depicted in Daniel 7 as: (1) *not* being one of the ten horns or kings, verses 8 and 20; (2) but as having to defeat three of the ten horns in order to gain his ascendancy in the West, verse 20; (3) and this same little horn, or number eleven, was the leader who made war even with the saints (cf. Rev 19:11-21), as verse 21 indicates.

Perhaps the reason so many have mistaken the Antichrist's origin in the political spectrum is that he was expected to be a Jew in order to make a covenant with the Jews (Dan 9:24-27). Or it may come from a gross failure to identify the whole seventieth week of Daniel as a period of wars, that is, as the Great Tribulation period (Rev 7:14).

But the Antichrist defeats three kings in the West before the first half of the seventieth week is over. In addition, he hears those tidings from the North (Dan 11:44) while he is battling the king of the South successfully. And just prior to the middle of the seventieth week, he defeats the king of the North (cf. Eze 38-39). With this battle, he becomes the top world leader. The kings of the East did not arrive at the time he got the tidings, probably because they could not cross over the Euphrates in that time (Rev 16:12-14) because the timing of the pouring out of God's bowls of wrath was not yet.

But the Antichrist will come to his end (Dan 11:45), and no one shall be able to give him help. He could not, as Antichrist, conquer the genuine Christ (Rev 19:11-21).

The image of the Gentile times, in Daniel 2, was a picture of the political arrangements from 600 BC until the second advent of the King of kings. Nebuchadnezzar was to reign "wherever the children of men dwell" (Dan 2:38). The

Greek ruler was to "bear rule over all the earth" (Dan 2:39). The rulers were all to be changed by God (behind the scenes), as Daniel 4:17 indicates clearly. This political scene was to show its increasing inferiority until the stone (the Messiah) struck the image, and in its place, the Messiah would fill the whole earth, having broken and consumed all preceding kingdoms (Dan 2:44). Interestingly, all of this was said to be a *secret* (Dan 2:47). It appears well kept, as far as unregenerate people are concerned. Unfortunately, some scholarly believers do not think the kingdom which the Messiah will bring to earth will have any political aspect. How then shall we understand the clear prophecy of God through Isaiah (2: 1-4):

> The word that Isaiah the son of Amoz saw concerning Judah and Jerusalem. And it shall come to pass in the last days, that the mountain of the LORD's house shall be established in the top of the mountains, and shall be exalted above the hills; and all nations shall flow unto it. And many people shall go and say, Come ye, and let us go up to the mountain . . . to the house of the God of Jacob; and he will teach us of his ways, and we will walk in his paths: for out of Zion shall go forth the law and the word of the LORD from Jerusalem. And he shall judge among the nations, and shall rebuke many people: and they shall beat their swords into plowshares, and their spears into pruninghooks: nation shall not lift up sword against nation, neither shall they learn war any more.

THE WORLD LOOKED AT RELIGIOUSLY

Everything started deteriorating on a major scale in Babylon. It was there that Nimrod performed as God's mighty rebel. It was there that the tower was built to deify humanism or humanity. It was there that there existed one world, a natural desire of man, as we have shown. It was there that God made it impossible for man to have one world apart from the Messiah as His everlasting King of kings reigning in the earthly realm. It was there that Babylonianism originated. It is Babylonianism that will rear its head the highest in the Great Tribulation period (Rev 17). This religious system is said in verse 5 to be a great mystery because it has mothered so many (550 plus) adulterous religions, cults, and sects. It is this kind of a religious system that the Antichrist will ride to his zenith. It is an eclectic mass of ideas—something for everybody—and much like a chameleon as it spreads across the world. I do not believe this is Romanism, although it may well be included. Dead Protestantism is in that potpourri as well. But it is into this kind of a religious time of the end that world prophecy predicts the world will come. The trends are all around us and picking up intensity. But the ends are not yet. The USA will have much to contribute to this religious smorgasbord, unfortunately.

THE WORLD LOOKED AT COMMERCIALLY

The eighteenth chapter of Revelation certainly depicts Babylonianism in its commercial aspect. It appears to this student of the Word that Daniel 11:40*c* indicates that the Antichrist passes over the land of Palestine to Babylon, perhaps, where he establishes the commercial mart spoken of in Revelation 18. Later, for religious reasons found in Revelation 13, he plants his palace in Jerusalem (Dan 11:45). At any rate, the Antichrist will capture the riches of the business world, for he must control the whole world indeed. It is not too extreme to say that the USA's advance in commercial enterprises provides yet another asset to the Western ruler for world conquest and control. This is perhaps one of the considerations that will force the ten nations to throw their entities to his disposal for his hour on the world horizon.

The reader can easily provide the volumes of information available today to substantiate the role of the West at any of these checkpoints: geography, politics, religion, or commerce.

But all of these factors, and more, are flowing faster and faster into a demonic vortex. The night is far spent (Ro 13: 11-13), and the day's dawn is drawing nearer. What manner of men ought we to be in the light of these things? Certainly we must grow an even greater respect for the predictive Word of God than ever before. This will keep us individually headed for the winning goal.

Unfortunately, it is necessary to look upon that great climactic scene of the final Tribulation-period Battle of Armageddon and anticipate that the whole world will be there, including the USA.

The classic passages dealing with the final gathering of the nations of the world during the times of the Gentiles are Psalm 2 and Revelation 19. As we close this study of America and world prophecy, we should observe the great difficulty into which the Antichrist gets the nations, and they do not appear to have protested at all.

Psalm 2 puts matters in a philosophic framework. "*Why* do the [nations] rage, and the people imagine a vain [empty] thing?" (v. 1, italics added).

Revelation 19 puts matters in the framework of a robed bride returning with a conquering Bridegroom to reign on earth. All of them are dressed in white. The only thing standing out from the white are the dried Calvary bloodstains on His vesture. But perhaps even they are overprinted or surrounded by the notes of Calvary victory, King of kings and Lord of lords.

What is it that the Antichrist has led the nations to do? He has successfully sold them on coming to Israel's Armageddon battlefield to intercept the returning Messiah. Since the devil was not able to defeat Christ at His first advent, he makes this massive worldwide attack as formidable as is possible. I believe, on the basis of Matthew 24:29-30 and Psalm 2:4, that the Messiah will be sitting in the clouds for some time while He pleads to the Antichrist below that the latter let His people Israel go from the nations represented. It is like Moses and Pharaoh long ago.

So, contrary to some nineteenth-century opinion, this Battle of Armageddon is not international strife of one nation against the other, but the whole world of nations against the soon coming King of all kings. It is a major, worldwide event. All the world will be there. No believers will be at Armageddon to battle the Messiah. But there are massive numbers of unbelievers in our world today—yes, unfortunately in our USA. They will be there.

And what does the Antichrist suggest to the true Messiah? In the first place, he openly admits that he is opposed to the Lord and to His *Messiah* (Ps 2:2*b*). Second, he wants to cast the bands of both Father and Son from the nations. He has read God's prophetic Word. He knows Daniel chapter 4. He knows the time of Messiah's second advent from Daniel 9:26-27. He knows that it is Antichrist's last hope, unless he can pull his devious plan off.

The results are already prerecorded in the classic passages, especially in Revelation 19:11-21. Every single unbeliever will be wiped off the face of the earth, as in the days of Noah (Mt 24:37). A new national arrangement will come into being (Mt 25:31-46). The Messiah will be King of all kings. He will govern the nations with a rod of iron. His rule will bring a saturation of blessing no one and no world has ever seen before. America will be regenerated by grace through faith, pivoted upon the Americans of the Tribulation period who believe in the Messiah and who do not die. For they will enter the millennial realm of the Messiah, first because of salvation by grace, and, second, as a national bloc because they treated the Israelites in their midst properly during the Tribulation period.

The texts are there for your study and further discovery, and remember the knowledge of the book of Daniel will be increased as we read it (Dan 12:4).

9

EARLY AMERICA'S PORTRAIT OF GOD

Earl D. Radmacher

In response to the question, "What is America?" G. K. Chesterton replied, "A nation with the soul of a church"; that is, a nation founded upon a theological creed, whose articles confess the created equality of men under God, the ordination of governments to assure justice to all, and the overarching belief in the Creator as source and final authority from whom these blessings and all other derivative privileges come. Chesterton's phrase is an apt one, for it calls attention to America's overwhelmingly religious past. It evokes the pleasant recall and sober reflection of this nation's unique beginnings, those one hundred fifty odd years which ranged from Plymouth to Lexington, a period of unparalleled opportunity, privilege, and responsibility, as viewed through largely Puritan lenses. To understand Chesterton's phrase, we must rewind the reel which portrays the mind and heart, the sinew and muscle of early America, of Puritan America.

Recent issues of *The History Teacher,* a journal for historians, have presented three articles which contain a compilation of scores of definitions for the meaning of history. Indeed, history has been defined in a variety of ways, from the sarcastic to the humorous, from the cynical to the sober. However defined, history, as recorded, begins as words on a page.

But what are behind those words? What suffering, what achievement, what defeat, what glory? What do the words of Scripture reveal—reflect—recall? Think with me of an obituary notice in a day's newspaper, a few short lines, an exceedingly brief recapitulation of the essential data, terminal dates, next of kin.

But, again, what volumes are hidden behind this teasingly limited capsule of information!

"A nation with the soul of a church." Who created the soul? Who gave it its character? Which events transpired to venture upon such a noble experiment? From where? By whom? And why? It has been said that history is made, not by political, economic, and social leaders, but by ordinary people, who, by their character and beliefs, largely determine their leadership. In early America, these people were Puritans in their institutions, culture, morals, and beliefs. If one chose not to join himself to the society of visible saints, he was obliged, nevertheless, by the nature of the existing commonwealth, at least in Massachusetts Bay, to be a part of the reigning Puritan culture.

In an article written more than a half-century ago, Charles A. Beard, no friend of the Puritans, made a listing of terms used to describe these early Americans, terms garnered from the writings of both friends and enemies. One list included: *godliness, thrift, industry, temperance, principle, holy Sabbath, self-government.* The other list, somewhat more darkly, plumped for *Philistinism, sour-faced fanaticism, supreme hypocrisy, demonology, intellectual tyranny, brutal intolerance grisly sermons,* and *bigotry.*[1]

If these negative evaluations are essentially correct, one may wonder how such a people, with their philosophy and codes of life, could prepare thirteen colonies to forge the United States of America. The new republic was the product of its own culture, however symbiotic, a culture yet existing under the aegis, even in 1776, of Puritan thought categories. Granting the contributions of enlightenment and humanist ideas, and fully cognizant of its abysmal misconceptions and errors, it was the moral force of Puritanism which gave to the new nation its capacity to grow, to expand, and to endure in freedom. Historian Ralph Barton Perry encounters the question of their contributions with this positive note: "The Puritans imprinted on American . . . institutions a quality of manly courage, self-reliance, and sobriety. We are still drawing upon the resources of spiritual vigor which they accumulated."[2]

Ralph Waldo Emerson, in order to make a point, declared, "There is properly no history; only biography," which brings us back to people. What sort of people were the Pilgrims who founded Plymouth Colony and their nonseparating Puritan counterparts who settled Massachusetts Bay Colony?

Their high view of God and of His providential concern with their affairs is mirrored over and over again in Governor William Bradford's liberty monument, *Of Plymouth Plantation:* "They knew that they were Pilgrims and looked not much on those things, but lifted up their eyes to heaven their dearest country, and quieted their spirits."[3] "So they grew in knowledge, and other gifts and graces of the Spirit of God; and lived together in peace, and love, and holiness."[4] "It may be spoken to the honor of God and without prejudice to any, that such was the true piety, the humble zeal and fervent love of this people . . . towards God and His ways, and the single-heartedness and sincere affection one toward another, that they came as near the primitive pattern of the first churches as any other church of these later times have done, according to their rank and quality."[5]

Bradford's classic account speaks further of their "just God," committing "themselves to the will of God," and entering Cape Cod Harbor "by God's good providence." Recalling this latter experience with a sense of happy and praiseful relief, Bradford says that "being thus arrived in a good harbor, and brought safe to land, they fell upon their knees and blessed the God of heaven who had brought them over the vast and furious ocean and delivered them from all the perils and miseries thereof, again to set their feet on the firm and stable earth, their proper element."[6]

And of what sort were the builders of the Bay Colony? Robert Baird observes that Governor John Winthrop and his fellow passengers to America were "almost without exception godly people." The irenic and noble spirit of these voyagers to America rises from the pages of a letter written by Winthrop to his fellow Anglicans, in which he calmly requests their fervent prayers for a safe journey:

> We conceive much hope that this remembrance of us, if it be frequent and fervent, will be a most prosperous gale in our sails and provide such a passage and welcome for us from the God of the whole earth, as both we which shall find it, and yourselves . . . shall be much enlarged to bring in such daily returns of thanksgivings, as the specialties of his Providence and goodness may justly challenge at all our hands . . . let the . . . Spirit put you in mind that are the Lord's remembrances, to pray for us without ceasing . . . making continual request for us to God in all your prayers.[7]

The letter continues with a spirit of prayerful reciprocation:

> What goodness you shall extend to us on this or any other Christian kindness, we, your brethren in Christ Jesus, shall labor to repay in what duty we are or shall be able to perform, promising so far as God shall enable us, to give him no rest on your behalf, wishing our heads and hearts may be as fountains of tears for your everlasting welfare, when we shall be in our poor cottages in the wilderness, overshadowed with the spirit of supplication, through the manifold necessities and tribulations which may not altogether unexpectedly, nor we hope, unprofitably befall us. And so commending you to the grace of God in Christ, we shall ever rest.[8]

The observation is well placed which says, "The challenge which the Puritan met was to provide an environment conducive to the effective transmission of the Old World to the New, no-easy task."[9] That such a challenge, by this kind of people, was even considered and successfully undertaken, bespeaks of their tough-minded belief in God with a unique sense of calling. Professor Ahlstrom of Yale makes the flat statement: "The architects of the 'Puritan Way,' therefore, were in a very real sense the founders of the American nation."[10]

From the writings of men of their own time and of modern historians with sufficient scientific objectivity to face these early Americans squarely, we have suggested something of the character of this people. But now, let us advance a bit further into the Puritan makeup, which provided the impulse to move to America from England.

The Puritan Impulse Toward America

Of the several factors which have helped to make America,

> Puritanism has been perhaps the most conspicuous, the most sustained, and the most fecund. Its role in American thought has been almost the dominant one, for the descendants of Puritans have carried at least some habits of the Puritan mind into a variety of pursuits, have spread across the country, and in many fields of activity have played a leading part. The force of Puritanism . . . has been accentuated because it was the first of these traditions to be fully articulated, and because it has inspired certain traits which have persisted long after the vanishing of the original creed. Without some understanding of Puritanism, it may safely be said, there is no understanding of America.[11]

Of these "habits of the Puritan mind" which have inspired certain persistent traits, may I focus on three: their vocation, moral conscience, and individuality.

These transplanted Englishmen and Englishwomen seemingly knew nothing about leisure or idleness, at least not in the earlier years of their experiment. After all, a wilderness required taming, houses needed building, laws needed formulating, Indians must be befriended, towns must be laid out, schools and colleges founded. From the inner reserves of the divinely imparted motivation, and confident of the rightness, and indeed the necessity, of their appointed task, the Puritans worked with zest and exhilaration. In the face of privations, which, to the modern reader seem almost innumerable and, in their consequences, incalculable, a holy disinterestedness as to self marked their labors, for they were members of Massachusetts Bay Colony, a commonwealth which bore the inscription: "A due form of government, both civil and ecclesiastical." Perry Miller has written, "Existence for him was completely dramatic; every minute was charged with meaning."[12]

These builders of a colony were first and foremost men and women of integrity—of necessity, for all work was contracted with a glorious and triumphant eternity in view. Work had been ordained by the almighty Creator and hence was accepted with a sense of mission, whether the synodical struggles of a controverted antinomianism or the daily chores of a humble housewife. Idleness, thus, was a chief violation of civil and religious law and met with punishments unduly severe to us today. This pulsating, lively sense of a calling led one historian to describe the Puritan as "a visionary who never forgot that 2+2=4; he was a soldier of Jehovah who never came out on the losing side of a bargain. He was a radical and a revolutionary, but not an anarchist; he ruled with an iron hand, and also according to fundamental law. He was a practical idealist, with a strong dash of cynicism."[13]

Not unrelated to his sense of vocation was the mind set which viewed all of life with a most serious demeanor. Convictions were held about everything: work, dress, entertainments, ethics, worship, music, education. There were no allowable exceptions. Every event was accepted as Providential.

Each man endeavored to treat his neighbor as Christ would. Each was forever preoccupied with conformity to biblical injunctions, hence, ever alert to the signs of an evil presence. A realist to the core, "He refused to ignore or to sentimentalize the pain, the labor, the misery . . . the imminence of death" which dogged his steps.[14] As a "moral athlete," the Puritan "made a business of moral virtue, felt his spiritual pulse, took his spiritual weight, and measured his spiritual record."[15]

Cotton Mather shows how such disciplinary exercise might be done:

> What is there that I may do for the service of the glorious Lord, and for the welfare of those for whom I ought to be concerned?
>
> Having implored the direction of God . . . consider the matter . . . till you have resolved on something. Write down your resolutions. Examine what precept and what promise you can find in the Word of God to countenance your resolutions. Review these memorials at proper seasons, and see how far you have proceeded in the execution of them. The advantages of these . . . memorials no rhetoric will be sufficient to commend, no arithmetic to calculate. There are some animals of which we say, "They know not their own strength;" Christians, why should you be like them?[16]

Unlike other colonists in other places around the world, the Puritans made no concessions to their wilderness. Despite the savage conditions of their physical environment, they built and maintained village schools and a notable college, in order that their children might enjoy a literate ministry "when our present ministers shall lie in the dust." The Puritan mind was one of the toughest the world has ever had to deal with. It is impossible to conceive of a disillusioned Puritan; no matter what misfortune befell him, no matter how often or how tragically his fellowman failed him, he would have been prepared for the worst and would have expected no better.[17] Yet he was by no means a fatalist, for God was in complete control of all events. He was neither lukewarm nor halfhearted.

The strong-minded individualism, however, must not be construed as insular, for the Puritans were a covenant people; such covenantism forbade self-seeking. Indeed, their covenant theology, as understood and practiced, served as the ground of all their hopes and faith and labors. As God entered into covenants with Adam, Abraham, and Moses, so with these seventeenth-century children of Zion. By virtue of the covenant conditions, God dealt with His elect. By means of the covenant principle, churches, commonwealths, and constitutions were formed. Civil and ecclesiastical concerns arose from out of the covenant. The Mayflower Compact is a notable example. Thus, the Puritans brought together their energetic, rock-ribbed individualism and a corporate sense in extraordinary combination.

The Puritan character thus selectively described was, of course, the fruit of Reformation tenets, without which Puritanism would have had no existence whatsoever. Among their unquestioned doctrines were the sole authority of Scripture and belief in a sovereign God.

The Bible was the superlative, incomparable Book. The Puritans treasured their Bibles as the most valued of their possessions, viewing them not as a collection of sacred documents but as the full disclosure of the will and ways of God. Their speech, their towns, their children's names, their expressions reflected the pervasive hold of the scriptural text upon their everyday thinking. The Bible was the perfect rule. Its authority superseded all other authorities, especially that of the papal church and all ecclesiastical tradition. To know and to do God's will, they said, one must know the Bible well. Samuel Willard of the Old South Church in Boston declared the Bible to be the "only touch stone" for faith and practice, and "whatsoever doctrines are not according to it, are to be repudiated as false." It was an infallible, unified, trustworthy guide: "Every Truth agrees with the whole and with every other Truth."[18] Although God's providential workings were continuously being exhibited in the natural world, He gave no commands to the consciousness of men apart from the biblical record; hence, the Puritan hatred of all forms of quietism and enthusiasm.

The entire universe was held to be under the direct continuous controlling guidance of God. Though effects were seemingly produced by "secondary causes," the actual government of all events, from the setting of the sun at dusk to the blossoming of the most insignificant flower, was under His superintendence. To ascribe effects to change or to nature was to miss altogether a vision of the dynamic hand of God. These words of a New England parson were often heard in village meeting houses: "The whole administration of Providence in the upholding and government of all created beings, in a way of highest wisdom and exact order, it is *all* His work. . . . Those notable changes in the world in the promoting or suppressing, exalting or bringing down of Kingdoms, Nations, Provinces, or Persons, they are all wrought by Him."[19]

John Davenport, a founder of the New Haven Colony, included in his creed the following article: God having made all things, "as a faithful Creator doth still uphold, dispose, and govern all things to the ends for which they were created, having care especially for man, and amongst men, chiefly for the righteous and believers; so that neither good nor evil befalls any man without God's providence."[20]

Governor Bradford's record of the Pilgrim odyssey is a testimonial gem to the Puritan's confidence in God's right ordering of events, no matter how adverse. Fervent prayers preceded every decision, for they knew all things were cupped in His hands. Upon their departure from England to Holland, "They rested on His providence, and knew whom they had believed."[21] And again: "But when man's hope and help wholly failed, the Lord's power and mercy appeared in their recovery . . . with fervent prayers they cried unto the Lord in this great distress . . . yet Lord Thou canst save! Yet Lord Thou canst save."[22]

After some eleven years in exile, John Robinson's Pilgrim congregation pondered carefully their next major move. The Dutch had been very kind to them; yet Holland was but an asylum. The Pilgrim parents feared for their children's futures; and all were troubled over the resumption of hostilities by Catholic Spain and the newly independent northern provinces. Bradford writes, "And first, after their humble prayers to God for His direction and assistance . . . they consulted what particular place to . . . prepare for."[23]

More than a century later, in a small Massachusetts village, during a period of religious awakening, a Congregational minister reiterated in a series of sermons these same sentiments. God's activity was not limited only to the daily concerns of His elect, but, at the same time, to a "great design" encompassing His work of redemption throughout the whole world. In 1739, Jonathan Edwards said, "History consists of many successive marks and dispensations of God, all tending to one great effect . . . and all together making up one great work." In this redemptive work, nothing was viewed as either fortuitous or accidental. Dividing the Christian era into several parts, he envisioned the final defeat of Satan and a Millennial glory within history preceding Christ's return. Heresy and error were to vanish. America and the whole earth would soon radiate with glorious Gospel light and Christian love. Hopefully, this glory would begin to be revealed in America (the "isles" of Is 60:9).[24] Whatever our eschatological hopes, the overiding motif in Edwards' postmillennialism was: Christ is King; Satan's days are numbered; God's grand purposes will achieve realization; "So that the whole is *of* God, and *in* God, and *to* God, and God is the beginning, middle, and end in this affair."[25]

Here, then, were people who exuded supreme confidence in

their calling, faith, covenants, hope, for all was from God, their universal, immutable, eternal, invisible, and loving Sovereign. How many times they had occasion to reflect upon His compassionate concern for His own, "filling their afflicted minds with such comforts as everyone cannot understand."[26]

Their unshakable confidence appears in this memorial of Bradford, written after the Pilgrims' arrival at Plymouth: "May not and ought not the children of these fathers rightly say: Our Fathers were Englishmen which came over this great ocean, and were ready to perish in this wilderness; but they cried unto the Lord, and He heard their voice and looked on their adversity."[27]

The Puritan Migration: Privilege and Responsibility

In reviewing the character and beliefs of our Puritan forefathers, we have had occasion to hear them speak to us from their experiences, an unwanted and harried people, seeking a place of settlement, to live and worship according to the Word. But how did they see themselves and their grand adventure? As a bedraggled bunch of troublemakers, aimlessly wandering about from place to place, or as a congregation of God's saints, under His care, pursuing a divine commission? Let us hear them speak again. As they prepared to leave Plymouth, England, in late summer of 1620, Bradford offered a clue: "And thus, like Gideon's army, this small number was divided, as if the Lord by this work of His providence thought these few too many for the great work He had to do."[28]

What was this "great work"? In "A Model of Christian Charity" (note the word *Model*), Governor John Winthrop gave a clear answer. They had entered into a covenant with God, as "a Company professing ourselves fellowmembers of Christ . . . by a mutual consent through a special overruling providence . . . to seek out a place of cohabitation and consorteship under a due form of government both civil and ecclesiastical." That is, to establish a biblical church polity and a biblical civil society, the magistrates undergirding the churches and the ministers supporting the commonwealth. Winthrop continued: "The end is to improve our lives to do more service to the Lord, to increase the body of Christ whereof we are members, and that our posterity may be better preserved from the common corruptions of this evil world." To accomplish these ends, extraordinary means must be employed. Profession must be transposed to "constant practice." Love must proceed from "a pure heart fervently; we must bear one another's burdens, etc."[29]

Their "errand" was to purify the visible Church by purging from it popish and all other anti-Christian remains, according to Reformed doctrines of discipline and piety, the office of the Christian magistrate assisting. In short, to bring God's judgments and order to all people, especially to the Church. The Puritan fathers found their inspiration for such an ambitious enterprise in Scripture. There they learned that man is to be a fruitful member on God's earth; governments and laws are instituted to restrain sin. The Old Testament especially gave clear instructions on one's personal life, the proper ordering of a community, and the revitalizing of the Church. The Puritan demanded "a revolution of the saints."[30]

"Their errand was not a mere scouting expedition: it was an essential maneuver in the drama of Christendom. The Bay Company was not a battered remnant . . . thrown upon a rocky shore; it was an organized task force of Christians, executing a flank attack on the corruptions of Christendom."[31] Their intent was to build a Zion in New England for all Europe and the world to copy.

That these resolute Englishmen were aware of the significant ramifications of their God-given opportunity is revealed in this classic paragraph from Bradford's *History*: "All great and honorable actions are accompanied with great difficulties and must be both enterprised and overcome with answerable courages. . . . Their condition was not ordinary, their ends were good and honorable, their calling lawful and urgent; and therefore they might expect the blessing of God on their proceedings."[32]

As with every kind of genuine opportunity and privilege, especially of a spiritual kind, responsibility is a necessary accompaniment. No one knew this better than these Puritan leaders and their fellow colonists. From the very commencement of the Great Migration, the consequences of failure were drummed into their remembrances. "When God gives a special commission He looks to have it strictly observed in every Article." Did not Saul lose his kingdom through disobedience? "We are entered into covenant with Him for this work, we have taken out a commission; we have professed to enterprise these actions upon these and these ends; we have hereupon besought him of favor and blessing."

Should these people neglect their calling, dissemble with God, become materialistic and carnal in their pursuits, "The Lord will surely breakout in wrath vs. us and be revenged of such a perjured people, and make us know the price of the breach of such a covenant." They must follow the counsel of Micah to walk humbly, they must "be willing to abridge ourselves of our superfluities for the supply of others' necessities . . . we must delight in each other."

> If we shall deal falsely with our God in this work we have undertaken and so cause him to withdraw his present help from us, we shall be made a story and a byword through the world. We shall open the mouths of enemies to speak evil of the ways of God . . . ; we shall shame the faces of many of God's worthy servants and cause their prayers to be turned into curses upon us till we be consumed out of the good land where we are going. . . . If our hearts shall turn away so that we will not obey, but shall be seduced and worship other gods . . . and serve them, it is propounded unto us this day, we shall surely perish out of the good land whether we pass

> over this vast sea to possess it. Therefore, let us choose life, that we and our seed may live; by obeying his voice and cleaving to him, for he is our life and our prosperity.[33]

And finally, the admonition of a seventeenth-century Puritan: "If we should so frustrate and deceive the Lord's expectations, that His covenant interest in us, and the workings of His salvation be made to cease, then all were lost indeed; Ruin upon ruin, destruction upon destruction would come, until one stone were not left upon another."[34]

We have noted the character and beliefs which provided the Puritan impulse toward America. We have read their estimate of the cosmic significance of their holy commission, its privileges and responsibilities. In conclusion, we may ask properly, Who are their descendants? Who follow in their train? Who know and care enough about these things even to give some consideration to these questions? George Santayana observed, "A country without a memory is a country of madmen." It has also been said, "History repeats itself because no one was listening the first time." How many are "listening" to the history of early America—obeying our commission, working with vigor while morally alert, bearing the pain and hardship of building with Christ His Church within a biblical and strategic mental framework, holding always before our vision the greater weight of eternal glory?

How many will believe as they? Over the centuries, the number has decreased. How has this come to pass? Ralph Barton Perry offers this answer:

> Because the critic frankly takes the side of Mammon and recognizes the puritan as his enemy. His criticism is self-defense or counter attack. . . . Everyone will . . . confess his lapses from strict rectitude. But one dislikes to be perpetually reminded of these things. When a puritan is in the neighborhood, one feels the uncomfortable sense of an accusing presence. It is impossible to go on enjoying oneself frivolously in the midst of such gravity. The puritan . . .

> cannot be lightly ignored, because his admonition is re-echoed and confirmed by one's own conscience. . . . Hence one hurls epithets at the puritan, hoping to frighten him away; or, if not, then to divert his attention and put him on the defensive by calling to his own shortcomings.[35]

Even the best of the Puritan way of life, to which we have addressed ourselves, is an unwanted, unsold commodity today. Because in their more biblical moments, these earliest colonists reflected biblical revelations and injunctions, Americans for the most part have lost their taste and appreciation of Puritan manners. As L. P. Hartley wryly put it: "The past is a foreign country; they do things differently there." Indeed, "History has a way of censoring contemporary values."

As Puritan opportunities and responsibilities were as great as their faith and their God—for One was the source of the others—so those whose faith and whose God are essentially the same face, in this Bicentennial year of 1976, equally great opportunities and responsibilities. How shall we respond? How alert are we to the consequences of failure?

On June 12, 1775, the Continental Congress dispatched from Philadelphia to the thirteen colonies a recommendation that July 20 be observed as "a day of publick humiliation, fasting, and prayer." Why? Because God "frequently influences the minds of men to serve the wise and gracious purposes of his providential government . . . especially in times of impending danger and publick calamity."

What was the nature of this prayerful petition? "That we may with united hearts and voices unfeignedly confess and deplore our many sins, and offer up our joint supplications to the all-wise, omnipotent, and merciful Disposer of all events; humbly beseeching him to forgive our iniquities, to remove our present calamities, to avert those desolating judgments with which we are threatened."[36]

Following the example of 150 years of colonial practice, in the face of threatened war, seeking from God a redress of the many grievances which had troubled the colonies on a wide scale, the assembled representatives instinctively (?) realized that a deeper search of their own souls was required as "the indispensable prologue" to divine intervention.[37]

Buckle reflected that "there will always be a connection between the way men contemplate the past and the way in which they contemplate the present." Whatever else may be said of our nation's founders, this much we must affirm: the example of the Congress in 1775 is worthy of national emulation.

NOTES

1. Charles A. Beard, "On Puritans," in *New Republic,* December 1920, pp. 15-17.
2. Ralph B. Perry, *Puritanism and Democracy* (New York: Harper & Row, 1944), Harper Torchbooks, p. 268.
3. William Bradford, *Of Plymouth Plantation,* ed. Samuel E. Morrison, (New York: Knopf, 1975), p. 47.
4. Ibid., p. 17.
5. Ibid., p. 19.
6. Ibid., pp. 58-61.
7. Robert Baird, *Religion in the United States of America* (New York: Arno Press and *The New York Times,* 1969), p. 108.
8. Ibid., p. 109.
9. George M. Walker, ed., *Pioneer Early America* (Boston: Heath, 1950), paperback ed., p. viii.
10. Sydney A. Ahlstrom, "Theology in America: A Historical Survey," in *The Shaping of American Religion,* ed. J. W. Smith, and A. L. Jamison (Princeton: U. Press, 1969), 1: paperback ed., 236.
11. Perry Miller, "The Puritan Way of Life," in *Puritanism in America,* ed. George M. Walker (Boston: Heath, 1950), paperback ed., p. 4.
12. Ibid., p. 20.
13. Ibid.
14. Ralph B. Perry, "The Moral Athlete," in *Puritanism in America,* p. 100.
15. Ibid., p. 102.
16. Ibid.
17. Miller, p. 19.
18. Seymour Van Dyken, *Samuel Willard, 1640-1707: Preacher of Orthodoxy in an Era of Change* (Grand Rapids: Eerdmans, 1972), p. 41.
19. Miller, p. 9.
20. H. Shelton Smith; Robert T. Handy; & Lefferts A. Loetscher, *American Christianity,* (New York: Scribner's, 1960), 1:108-109.
21. Bradford, p. 13.
22. Ibid.
23. Ibid., p. 28.
24. These Millennial views are enlarged in Edwards' *History of the Work of Redemption.*

25. Jonathan Edwards, "Dissertation Concerning the End for Which God Created the World," quoted by Sydney A. Ahlstrom, *A Religious History of the American People* (New Haven: Yale U. Press, 1972), p. 310.
26. Bradford, p. 13.
27. Ibid., p. 63.
28. Bradford, p. 53.
29. Smith, Handy, & Loetscher, 1:98-102, passim.
30. Ahlstrom, *A Religious History of the American People*, p. 129.
31. Perry Miller, *Errand into the Wilderness* (New York: Harper & Row, 1964), Harper Torchbooks, p. 11.
32. Bradford, p. 27.
33. Smith, Handy, & Loetscher, 1:98-102, passim.
34. Miller, p. 6.
35. Perry, "The Moral Athlete," p. 105.
36. Perry Miller, "From the Covenant to the Revival," in *The Shaping of American Religion*, ed. Smith and Jamison, p. 322.
37. Ibid., p. 323.

10

LIBERTY AND FREEDOM IN THE OLD TESTAMENT

Earl D. Radmacher

Ever since Adam forfeited the obedience-oriented way of life and replaced it with the rebel-oriented way of lust (Gen 3:6), man has been constantly struggling for freedom. The rebel began running from God, and he reached disunity, strife, hate, immorality, murder. Instead of achieving the total freedom he anticipated, Adam was plunged into the darkness of depravity. His irresponsible act of selfishness toppled his human descendants into a dungeon of spiritual slavery.

God had given the first family tremendous freedom: unimpaired fellowship, direct communication, and untainted environment. Man had the freedom and power to multiply and fill the earth. Furthermore, God allowed him to rule as His vice-regent in that He gave him "dominion over the fish of the sea, and over the fowl of the air, and over every living thing that moveth upon the face of the earth." In addition, he had freedom to eat of "every seed-bearing herb on the face of all the earth, and every tree on which there are fruits containing seed."

This liberty and high privilege, however, carried, of necessity, a commensurately high standard of responsibility. God desired that man should exercise his creative capacity of choice in obedience. Thus, He graciously provided one tree of which man was not to eat. How simple and uncomplicated! God desired that man *obey*. But man desired to *rebel*. These two lifestyles—obedience or rebellion—have marked all human behavior since the Fall of man. At any point in time, a person, state, or nation, places allegiance in what God says to do (His Word) or in what man wants to do (his sin). One road leads to liberty and freedom; the other leads to slavery and imprisonment.

Let us draw four principles from the Old Testament with regard to liberty and freedom: (1) liberty is a covenant blessing, something that God promises to maintain as long as His people are faithful; (2) liberty is achieved only through bondage to the Creator God; (3) liberty allows man to serve God and thus find perfect freedom; (4) liberty releases high privileges that beget responsibility and thus accountability.

Liberty Is a Covenant Blessing

J. I. Packer of Trinity College, Bristol, defines liberty as "the happy state of having been released from servitude for a life of enjoyment and satisfaction that was not possible before."[1] In applying this to Israel in the Old Testament, he explains, "Liberty . . . means, on the one hand, deliverance from created forces that would keep men from serving and enjoying their Creator, and, on the other hand, the positive happiness of living in fellowship with God *under His covenant* [italics mine] in the place where He is pleased to manifest Himself and to bless."[2]

Abraham is a classic example of this in Genesis 12. Genesis 1-11 had shown us the problem of the world, that man is a rebel and runaway from God. But God, the "Hound of Heaven," tracks down a wealthy runaway rebel, Abram, to rescue him from his bondage. How fitting that God should go to Ur of the Chaldeans, "the seat of a vigorous polytheism whose uncontested master was Nanna (or Sin), the Sumero-

Akkadian moon god."[3] God chooses a man enslaved in pagan worship and offers him true liberty. Genesis 12:1-3 records the exceedingly great promise whereby Abram and his seed would be the vehicle of deliverance and blessing for all nations. "Now the LORD had said unto Abram, Get thee out of thy country, and from thy kindred, and from thy father's house, unto a land that I will show thee: And I will make of thee a great nation, and I will bless thee, and make thy name great; and thou shalt be a blessing: And I will bless them that bless thee, and curse him that curseth thee: and in thee shall all families of the earth be blessed."

The rest of chapters 12 through 14 shows the sovereign grace of God at work, bringing Abram to the point of simple uncompromising faith in the promise of God, whereby he is no longer a rebel but a member of God's forever family (Gen 15:6). Then, at that point, God obligates Himself unconditionally in a solemn covenant. God made a promise with conditions to a rebel, but He unconditionally covenanted Himself with His child. G. H. Land notes:

> It is of special importance that Abraham had acquired righteousness by faith, that is, was accounted a righteous person, before God spoke of elevating His promise to the status of a covenant. Verse 6 precedes verse 18. Sovereigns do not make covenants with rebels. They may make promises to them, always upon the condition of submission but only after resumption of loyalty and obedience can the king enter into binding relations with the subject.[4]

The sovereign, gracious, unconditional nature of this covenant is highlighted in the strange ceremony described in Genesis 15:7-21, showing that it is He, and not Abram, who is playing the leading role. Robert Laurin summarizes the significance of this occasion:

> Apparently one method by which men confirmed an agreement in those days was to cut the bodies of certain animals in

> pieces, lay them in two rows, and then pass together through the parts. The implication was that they were calling upon themselves a similar fate if they failed to keep their word (cf. Jer. 34:18). But here something important takes place: God alone passes through the pieces (symbolized by the "smoking fire pot" and "flaming torch," 15:17). Abram takes the animals, splits the carcasses, and lays them in a row, and then God puts him in a deep sleep and performs the rite himself. By this we are told simply that God alone is able to bring the promise to fulfillment. Man is to have his part—faithful obedience—but God alone is the covenant-fulfiller.[5]

God unilaterally and unconditionally obligates Himself in grace. Even when the covenant is expounded by the rite of circumcision, the emphasis is on God's obligation. Mendenhall reminds us, "It is not often enough seen that no obligations are imposed upon Abraham. Circumcision is not originally an obligation, but a sign of the covenant. . . . It serves to identify the recipient (s) of the covenant, as well as to give a concrete indication that a covenant exists."[6]

Centuries later, after repeated affirmations, God says to David, "I have made a covenant with my chosen, I have sworn unto David my servant. . . . My mercy will I keep for him for evermore, and my covenant shall stand fast with him. . . . My loving-kindness will I not utterly take from him, nor suffer my faithfulness to fail. My covenant will I not break, nor alter the thing that is gone out of my lips" (Ps 89:3, 28, 33-34).

God has a purpose, and He will graciously, persistently, and sovereignly work at it until that purpose is fulfilled. As Packer states it, "Liberty is not man's own achievement, but a free gift of grace, something which apart from God's actions man does not possess at all."[7]

Liberty Through Bondage to God

It is one thing to have privileges, but it is quite another

thing to experience and enjoy your privileges. The enjoyment of liberty graciously provided by God requires submission to the Architect of the plan. Again, Packer states: "Man can enjoy release from bondage to the created only through bondage to his Creator."

Because no one knows this need better than God Himself, He provided for it by also promising His people that they would serve in slavery. "And he said unto Abram, Know of a surety that thy seed shall be a stranger in a land that is not theirs, and shall serve them; and they shall afflict them four hundred years" (Gen 15:13). Thus, when we enter the account in Exodus, Israel is in Egypt under oppression, just as God had promised. This is particularly described in Exodus 1:8-14. Then in Exodus 2:23-24 we read: "And it came to pass in process of time, that the king of Egypt died: and the children of Israel sighed by reason of the bondage, and they cried, and their cry came up unto God by reason of the bondage. And God heard their groaning, and God remembered his covenant with Abraham, with Isaac, and with Jacob."

Israel knew from firsthand experience what it meant to suffer in slavery. How very welcome, therefore, was the beautiful deliverance related in the early chapters of Exodus. Then, in Exodus 19:4 God says to Moses: "Ye have seen what I did unto the Egyptians, and how I bare you on eagles' wings, and brought you unto myself." Having demonstrated to Israel that He is the Lord God Almighty, that He is altogether able to perform what He purposes on their behalf, He now solicits a commitment from them. "Now therefore, if ye will obey my voice indeed, and keep my covenant, then ye shall be a peculiar treasure unto me above all people: for all the earth is mine: And ye shall be unto me a kingdom of priests, and an holy nation" (Ex 19:5-6).

What a unique and far-reaching privilege for this seed of Abraham. They were to be God's representative nation on the earth—a theocracy. Here would be an opportunity to express openly and demonstrably to all the world their unique relationship to God. But, as I stated earlier, in order to experience their position, there needed to be a commitment: "if ye will obey my voice indeed, and keep my covenant." Thus, "Moses came and called for the elders of the people, and laid before their faces all these words which the LORD commanded him. And all the people answered together, and said, All that the LORD hath spoken we will do" (Ex 19:7-8).

It is important at this point to note a striking contrast between Genesis 15 and Exodus 19. When God covenanted with Abram, He put Abram to sleep, and He alone "passed between those pieces," solemnizing that covenant whereby He unconditionally obligated Himself to fulfill His promise. Now, in Exodus 19, there is quite a different setting. The partner to this covenant, namely, Israel, is wide awake, and she is required to commit herself to God if she is to be allowed this unique expression of her position in God. The lesson in the contrast is clear. God will most certainly fulfill His promise irrespective of Israel's response, but Israel will only be able to enjoy the blessings of that privileged position as she practices obedience.

> At the Exodus God set Israel free from bondage in Egypt, in order that henceforth the nation might serve Him as His covenant people (Ex. xix. 3ff., xx. 1ff.; Lv. xxv. 55; cf. Is. xliii. 21). He brought them into the "land flowing with milk and honey" (Ex. iii. 8; cf. Nu. xiv. 7ff.; Dt. viii. 7ff.), settled them there, and undertook to maintain them in political independence and economic prosperity as long as they eschewed idolatry and kept His laws (Dt. xxviii. 1-14). This meant that Israel's freedom would not depend upon her own efforts in either the military or the political realm, but on the quality of her obedience to God. Her freedom was a supernatural blessing, Yahweh's gracious gift to His own covenant people; unmerited and, apart from Him, unattainable in the first instance, and now maintained only through

> His continued favour. Disobedience, whether in the form of religious impiety or social injustice, would result in the loss of freedom. God would judge His people by national disaster and enslavement (Dt. xxviii. 25, 47ff.; cf. Jdg. ii. 14 ff., iii. 7ff., 12ff., iv. 1ff., vi. 1ff.) ; He would raise up hostile powers against them, and would ultimately cause them to be deported into a land where no tokens of His favour could be expected (Dt. xxviii. 64ff.; Am. v; 2 Ki. xvii. 6-23; cf. Ps. cxxxvii. 1-4) .[8]

Thus, their representative privilege as God's mediatorial people on earth was conditional. And in this conditional privilege God was not simply being legalistic, but He was teaching a principle inherent in mankind, namely, obedience brings the blessings of liberty and disobedience brings the curses of slavery.

As we move through the Old Testament, we find God's faithfulness in implementing these principles. He promised them that He would be faithful to bless them and to curse them. In no place are the options more fully stated than in Deuteronomy 28 through 30 and summarized in these words:

> See, I have set before thee this day life and good, and death and evil; in that I command thee this day to love the LORD thy God, to walk in his ways, and to keep his commandments and his statutes and his judgments, that thou mayest live and multiply: and the LORD thy God shall bless thee in the land whither thou goest to possess it. But if thine heart turn away, so that thou wilt not hear, but shalt be drawn away, and worship other gods, and serve them; I denounce unto you this day, that ye shall surely perish, and that ye shall not prolong your days upon the land, whither thou passest over Jordan to go to possess it. I call heaven and earth to record this day against you, that I have set before you life and death, blessing and cursing: therefore choose life, that both thou and thy seed may live: that thou mayest love the LORD thy God, and that thou mayest obey

> his voice, and that thou mayest cleave unto him: for he is thy life, and the length of thy days; that thou mayest dwell in the land which the LORD sware unto thy fathers, to Abraham, to Isaac, and to Jacob, to give them (30:15-20).

In following the volatile history of Israel through the pages of Scripture, one charts the up-and-down inconsistency of the nation. While camping under the umbrella of God's covenantal blessing, Israel experiences the supernatural blessing of liberty. We read in 2 Samuel 7:10-11 (NASB; cf. Ps 89), as God sends a message by way of Nathan to David: "I will also appoint a place for my people Israel and will plant them, that they may live in their own place and not be disturbed again, nor will the wicked afflict them any more as formerly. . . and I will give you rest from all your enemies."

Out from under this protective covenant and blessing, however, Israel's history is marred by enslavement. The book of Judges records these acts of disobedienec and their predictable results: "The angel of the LORD . . . said, 'I brought you up out of Egypt and led you into the land which I have sworn to your fathers and I said, I will never break My covenant with you . . . But you have not obeyed Me; what is this you have done?' " (Judg 2:1-2, NASB).

As a result, the Lord raised up hostile powers against them. He ultimately scattered them into a land that would provide little favor (2 Ki 17:6-23; Amos 5).

God's promise that the throne of David would be established forever (2 Sa 7:16; Ps 89:28-29) and His covenant ultimately confirmed through King David, was nevertheless tempered by a grave ultimatum concerning disobedience in Psalm 89:30-32: "If his [David's] sons forsake My law, and do not walk in My judgments, if they violate My statutes, and do not keep My commandments, then I will visit their transgression with the rod, and their iniquity with stripes."

True biblical liberty takes place only in a bondslave relationship to God. Independence of God is equal to imprisonment; dependence on God is requisite to freedom. The key to biblical liberty is disciplined structured living. Structure alone brings freedom; discipline brings liberty.

Today's society tells us just the opposite. The Law of God as revealed in the Old Testament was issued to the people of Israel to express the holy, just, and good character of God. The response of the nation of Israel was so often reflected throughout the book of Judges: "Everyone did what was right in his own eyes." Without God, there is no ethical, moral, or spiritual compass. What held true in 1700 BC holds true in AD 1976.

Liberty and freedom are achieved only through bondage to the Creator God.

Liberty Allows Man to Serve God

God's work demands our response. There are two roads of service in any person's life: sin and righteousness. To respond to the divine gift of liberty is the willful acceptance of bond-service to God. Because prior incarceration is implied when talking about liberty in the Old Testament, freedom in this context would mean the "joyful state of having been released from bondage for a life of servitude not possible before."

Old and New Testament liberty is a license to serve, not to sin. The victory won over Satan, sin, the Law, and death—made possible through Jesus Christ—evokes a life of *love*. This love will be expressed, again, through obedience and responsible service when the individual or nation recognizes the unfathomable grace extended. The admonition in Deuteronomy 6:5 to "Love the LORD your God with all your heart and with all your soul and with all your might" (NASB) becomes a logical response to what He has done. David's lofty dedicatory prayer in 1 Chronicles 29 is a case in point. David recognizes the liberating power and majesty of the Lord (v. 11), admits his frailty in serving the gracious God of Israel (v. 14), and then asks for a perfect heart for Solomon, "to keep Thy commandments, Thy testimonies, and Thy statutes, and to do them all" (v. 19).

When the apostle James talked of the "law of liberty" (Ja 1:25; 2:12), he spoke of the highest of all laws: the "law of love" (Gal 5:13). It is this motivation that spurs self-sacrificing service for the good of all men. Ultimately, this service is out of a sense of gratitude for this free gift of grace called liberty.

One of the most sterling examples of this is found in the closing chapter of the Chronicles and continues in the book of Ezra. Under the evil rule of Zedekiah (2 Ch 36:11-12), the Lord sent the unfaithful priests and the rebelling Israelites into captivity. The wrath of the Lord was mighty. As the Chaldeans were used to slay many of the unfaithful Israelites, God sent the survivors into Babylonian slavery, thus fulfilling the prophecy of Jeremiah. The book of Ezra picks up with the decree from Cyrus, King of Persia, that all of God's people would be *released to serve* in rebuilding the Temple. Liberty allows men to serve God.

Another pointed example of being set at liberty to serve is seen in the life of Daniel. Nebuchadnezzar's decree to worship the golden image placed the "peoples, nations, and men of every language" (Dan 3:4) in a dilemma. Those that fell down and worshiped the idol were committing treason against the God of Israel and thus were enslaved to the wicked system of the king. Daniel's friends entrusted themselves to God and were delivered by the Lord.

Daniel 11:32 (NASB) captures the philosophy of this great warrior of God, "The people who know their God will display strength and take action."

The logical conclusion concerning man's ability to serve and please his Creator is that the Fall destroyed man's freedom to control his way to do right (Jer 10:23). Man's heart is desperately wicked (Jer 17:9). Without the power of God to control this absolute propensity to sin continually, there would be no bent toward serving His ends (Eze 18:30-31).

Faith without works is as dead in the Old Testament as it is in the New (Deu 13:3-4). As Gustav F. Oehler stated, "In every important affair of life the Israelite has to accomplish something which God demands."[9] Or, as Psalm 37:3 says, "Trust in the LORD, and do good." The significance of moral commitment appears at the outset of human history. The preredemptive covenant contained a working agreement (Gen 2:17). Even after the Fall, empowered by the grace that brought freedom, the demonstration of good works brought acceptance (Gen 4:7). Further, although God accomplishes the saving (e.g., from the Flood), man must submit in obedience to qualify (Noah still had to build the ark, Gen 6:14).

The Old Testament proffers a redeemed life marked by activity as well as purpose. In 1 Chronicles 22:16, David issues a charge to Solomon, "Arise therefore, and be doing, and the LORD will be with thee." The consecration is typical of the Old Testament as a whole. Shecaniah, in a repentant attitude before God, cries to the people of Israel, "Arise! . . . be courageous and act" (Ezra 10:4, NASB).

Nehemiah is another classic example of how God delights in the service of man. In Nehemiah 4:6, he says, "So built we the wall; and all the wall was joined together . . . for the people had a mind to work."

God's work demands our response: to take action and serve Him.

LIBERTY PRODUCES PRIVILEGE THAT BEGETS RESPONSIBILITY

Spiritual liberty must eventuate in moral conduct. The preparatory washings at Mt. Sinai were a sign of the sanctification of Israel. The unclean were to be forsaken (Deu 23:1-3). God's nation became the peculiarly elect from all the nations but had to remain holy, or separated from the profane (Lev 20:26).

To quote J. Barton Payne, "In Israel, every activity became sacred. For when a man's aim is that of conformity to the will of God, who executes moral righteousness for all, life cannot be divided between the secular and the sacred."[10]

To be chosen as God's representative nation on earth was a high privilege. They were, indeed, a "peculiar treasure." But with the announcement of their uniqueness, Israel was obliged to receive the commandment two verses later: "And you shall be . . . a holy nation."

Privilege brought with it responsibility!

Oehler states,

> The fundamental principle of the law, torah, "instruction," is expressed in the words, "Be ye holy, for I am holy," Leviticus 11:44f., 19:2; or more completely, 20:7, "Sanctify yourselves and be holy, for I am Jehovah your God." The impress of consecration to the holy God is to be stamped on the life of the Israelites in ordinances extending to all important relations and conditions.[11]

The motive behind keeping the Law of God was one of gratitude to Him for prosperity and liberty (Deu 8:6-10). It also meant that punishment would be avoided (Ex 23:22-27; Lev 26; Deu 28).

Furthermore, holy living finds no special dispensation. Since the Lord's moral nature is immutable, the ethical requirements revealed through Moses to Israel are equally pertinent to the Church today. Christ came not to destroy the Law. What was *right* then is *right* today—in 1976. Believers in both the old and the new dispensations are to be governed by the same moral will of God. Israel's love for God was expressed in obeying His comandments (Ex 19:8). The Church's reflection of love for God is mirrored in the same way: "And this is love, that we walk after His commandments" (2 Jn 6).

Indeed, it appears that there is a principle that we in America can well note in the history of Israel, namely, privilege begets responsibility. And the greater the privilege, the greater the responsibility.

In this regard, we witness a sobering fact in the history of Israel. If we trace the saga of God's chosen people through the Old Testament, we find the repeated disobedience of the nation and disregard for their privileged position. This pattern continues until Ezekiel prophesies the departure of "the glory" from Israel.

When we finally come to the parable of the householder in Matthew 21:33-43, we find Jesus telling the leaders of the nation, the chief priests and elders in the Temple, that He is going to take them out of their privileged position of mediatorial representation and give that position to a nation or people bringing forth the fruits of it (Mt 21:43).

This transfer of mediatorial privilege is clearly defined in 1 Peter 2:9-10 (NASB; in much the same words recorded in Ex 19:6): "But you are A CHOSEN RACE, A ROYAL PRIESTHOOD, A HOLY NATION, A PEOPLE FOR GOD'S OWN POSSESSION, that you may proclaim the excellencies of Him who has called you out of darkness into His marvelous light; for you once were NOT A PEOPLE but now you are THE PEOPLE OF GOD; you had NOT RECEIVED MERCY, but now you have RECEIVED MERCY."

All of this is woven together by the apostle Paul in Romans 11, where we have the picture of the olive tree. The natural branches, the Jews, were broken off, and the Gentiles were grafted in (Rom 11:19). Paul warns (v. 21) those Gentiles that, in the event that arrogance overtakes them, "God did not spare the natural branches, neither will He spare you" (NASB). Let the warning be sounded to Gentiles who largely compose the Church in America.

Representative John Anderson, Chairman of the House Republican Conference, sounds the all-inclusive prophetic call:

> Each and every individual in any and all periods of hu-

> man history is directly *responsible* to the Creator, God. And we are called upon by this God not only to acknowledge His being, but to *serve* Him by serving His justice and righteousness. He calls us not only to respect justice, and not only to abstain from evil, but to actively pursue justice.[12]

This responsibility is active. It is never passive. Is 1976 a time for retreat from the perplexing pressures and problems eminating from a godless world system? No, says Arizona's Congressman John Conlan:

> There are two basic philosophies worldwide. One starts with God and makes man the minor premise. The other starts with no god and makes man the major premise. Those who believe the latter have been trying to centralize government while we who believe God is primary have been asleep at the switch. The humanists have come a long way. The patient (America) is at a point where it can recover and go on to greater strengths, or it can succumb.[13]

Representative Albert Quie, from Minnesota, sounds a similar warning against passive involvement: "We're getting away from religious orientation in trying to be neutral. There's no way we can be neutral. If we were, there would be no moral development at all."[14]

Our nation was born in a revolution, not unlike that of Israel. The inspiration of early America was largely spiritual. Our earliest settlers came to this continent having fled from religious persecution in England and the Netherlands. De Tocqueville, writing in *Democracy in America,* penned over a century ago, "It must never be forgotten that religion gave birth to Anglo-Saxon society."[15]

Those people who came to America were not zealously concerned with governing wealth and building a great nation state. Rather they were chiefly concerned with establishing a community based upon the commands of God.

John Cotton, pastor of the Massachusetts Bay Colony, said,

"Purity, preserved in the church, will *preserve well-ordered* liberty *in the people.*"[16]

God gave to the early Pilgrims an opportunity to come to a land of new privilege and new position, where they could express their faith freely. Those privileges have begotten to us responsibilities which we are now taking rather lightly. Perhaps now is the time to refresh our thinking with some of the messages that were brought by early leaders, such as Lincoln and his Gettysburg Address, in order that "these honored dead shall not have died in vain."

May we not play fast and loose with the privileges that we have received by failing to bear up under the responsibilities. If God was willing to discipline the Jews for their lack of responsible actions, surely God can discipline America for its lack of responsible actions with regard to the privileges that we have.

For just as liberty and freedom in the Old Testament could never be taken for granted, neither can we presume on the continuation of freedom today. This gracious privilege should make us more than people of passive theological contemplation; it ought to open us into responsible action. Taking God at His Word, our actions will make a difference—in 1976. As Benjamin Franklin said, "He that shall introduce into public affairs the principles of primitive Christianity will change the face of the world."[17]

We dare not waste the grace of God. His work demands our response.

NOTES

1. *The New Bible Dictionary*, ed. J. Douglas (Grand Rapids: Eerdmans, 1962), p. 732.
2. Ibid.
3. Encyclopedia Britannica, Macropaedia, 1974, 1:12a.
4. G. H. Land, "God's Covenants Are Conditional," in *The Evangelical Quarterly* (Apr.-June 1958), p. 86.
5. Robert Laurin, "Significance of the Patriarchal Narratives," in *Christianity Today* (Dec. 22, 1967), p. 17.

6. G. Mendenhall, *Law and Covenant in Israel and the Ancient Near East,* The Biblical Colloquim, 1955, p. 36.
7. *The New Bible Dictionary* p. 733.
8. Ibid., p. 739.
9. Gustav F. Oehler, *Theology of the Old Testament,* trans. George E. Day (Grand Rapids: Zondervan, n. d.), p. 182.
10. J. Barton Payne, *The Theology of the Older Testament* (Grand Rapids: Zondervan, 1962), p. 321.
11. Oehler, p. 182.
12. James C. Hefley, and Edward E. Plowman, *Washington: Christians in the Corridors of Power* (Wheaton, Ill.: Tyndale, 1975), p. 119.
13. Ibid., p. 131.
14. Ibid.
15. Quoted by Mark O. Hatfield, *Conflict and Conscience* (Waco, Tex.: Word, 1971), p. 66.
16. Ibid., p. 68
17. Hefley and Plowman, p. 1.